More Than a
Conqueror

More Than a
Conqueror

JACKIE BROWN RIDDICK

ARPress
ILLUMINATING IDEAS
EMPOWERING VOICES

ARPress
45 Dan Road Suite 5
Canton MA 02021

Hotline: 1(888) 821-0229
Fax: 1(508) 545-7580

Ordering Information:

Quantity sales. Special discounts are available on quantity purchases by corporations, associations, and others. For details, contact the publisher at the address above.

Printed in the United States of America.

ISBN-13:   Softcover   979-8-89330-547-0
              eBook   979-8-89330-548-7

Library of Congress Control Number: 2024901160

TABLE OF CONTENTS

Introduction.. 1

Dedication 3

Acknowledgements.. 5

About The Author 7

    1. Family.. 9

    2. Youthful Learning... 25

    3. Puberty To Maturity 50

    4. Outclassed 66

    5. Tony Takes The Military Road 74

    6. A Change In Scenery 86

    7. Don't Whine About It... 96

    8. Still Connected 109

    9. The Other Storms 123

    10. The Winds Of Change 134

    11. The Last Mile Of The Way 143

INTRODUCTION

Life is such a gift. I appreciate it even more as the years pass. Some seasons of life are longer than others, but along the pathway every life has value. We must not view our mistake as the definition of our existence. We are greater than the sum of our mistakes. We have a story to tell and although it may not be rosy on every page, it is our story and that makes it valuable. It's our reality. I invite you in as I turn a few pages of my life and interpret the wisdom of family, friends, neighbors, and a no-nonsense mother. I remember when...

DEDICATION

To my mother, Yvonne Winslow Brown, who helped shape my consciousness; and to all the teachers of the world who inspire, provoke, excite, and instruct; I tip my hat to you with high respect. To those who have endured sicknesses and the hardships of life and allowed us to share your story, you are priceless jewels, more than your struggle. My mom was all of that to me.

ACKNOWLEDGEMENTS

I salute my Husband Phillip; sons: Phil Jr. and Stephen Michael (Mikey); grand-daughter Mikayla; and my sisters Denise, JoAnn, Stephanie, and Vanessa. As our family has grown since this book's inception, its' added joys include Kristen, Mikey's wife, his children: Mikayla, Kennedi, Stephen Jr. (Buddy), and Jeremiah; and Thatania, Phil's wife, and Phil III. My mother-in-law Eugenia has been such a precious gem to me. I am so thankful for my dad and all of my family (which includes Phillip's family and the church). Finally, I would not be here without the rich love of God which strengthens me daily. I must give him abundant thanks. Each day offers the opportunity to give love out of such a great heritage. I am so thankful for this love.

ABOUT THE AUTHOR

Jackie Brown Riddick is a native of Sunbury, North Carolina where she grew up in rural Gates County and attended public schools. She received a Bachelor of Arts from Livingstone College in Salisbury, NC. She is happily married and honors the sanctity of marriage as the loving wife to Phillip Riddick, Sr. for over 30 years, mother of two sons (Phil & Mikey), and grandmother of five. She has traveled to many lands, but insists that people are the same with like passions. She believes God loves us all and everyone has value. While sharing her experiences she hopes to empower others to thrive in their virtues and abilities, and simply enjoy life. She ministers alongside her husband, Phillip who is pastor. They currently live in Chesapeake, Virginia.

FAMILY

A photo album lay on the top of the table in the family room of my home. Other framed pictures of events, different occasions in my life and family surround me. While seated in a chair adjacent to the photo album, my eyes fastened on its cover. At a glance it reminded me of so many forgotten days locked away in the back of my mind. I began to think of a few of the photos inside. Now eager to remember those times, I picked up the album changing seats nestling back on the sofa overwhelmed with anticipation. I thumbed through the album pages quickly, but then without hesitation at a much slower pace looking at picture after picture thinking of the stories that enveloped them.

My mind raced back to those moments represented. Turning the pages, I smiled as I saw a picture of Mommy. Lying in her bed, she tried to hide her laughter and smile with the blanket that covered her neatly dressed bed. She could not cover before the picture snapped though she made many attempts to do so. She pulled the covers so tightly towards her face that she exposed her feet. I laughed as I remembered her chastisement for capturing that unprepared moment. Those were photos I loved to film. She knew she would see that picture again, and others would see it too.

Pages of memories unfolded in my hands. The memories brought joy and laughter. Before I knew it, I was lost in time and settled in to ride a roller coaster of emotions. Smiles ushered me to the next series of photos. Taking a deep breath, I relaxed my head and shoulders onto the sofa and closed my eyes for a moment. More thoughts of Mommy came to mind and I began to miss her immensely. I wanted to cry even through the smiles. It's been a while since I've seen her face, and I would not see her again. Continuing through the album I looked, laughed, and smiled until every picture had been scrutinized with accounts from yesteryear. I closed the album, but I remembered. Holding the album snugly to my chest and now with some hesitation, I placed that album back on the table. While taking hold of yet another photo album and viewing each page, I was stuck with the image of Mommy in her bed and how hard we laughed that morning together. I remembered my yesteryear.

Mommy was a short woman about five feet two inches. Even with the small stature, she had a big heart of love that made her stand ten feet tall. Her laughter was electrifying. It was loud and hearty when she was tickled way deep down in her soul. She would throw her head back as her joy rang from some special place. Other times her laughter was softer bringing little or no attention when surrounded by a more conservative atmosphere. I missed her laughter. I simply missed Mommy.

She was the youngest child in her family of five children. The eldest of the children died of a childhood disease before Mommy was born. Raised with two sisters and one brother, she admired and looked up to all of them. They were very much a part of her adult life and our daily lives as we lived in a nearby community. We visited my grandparents practically every weekend while Mommy spoke to them daily. Nevertheless, Mommy did not talk about her childhood. I think it was a parenting tactic.

Now in our home, there were seven of us for most of my childhood. That included my parents, the four children, and my grandmother Anna. My parents had four children together—three girls and a boy. Although we liked to think there was something unusually brilliant about the four of us, we were similar to most of the kids we knew. Two parent homes were commonplace. Denise was the eldest child with deep dimples and an infectious smile. Antonio, whom we called Tony, was the watchful big brother to the bunch though not the oldest. I was the third child, and a tomboy. JoAnn was the cherished baby of the bunch. Everyone had to look out for the baby. There were only eleven months between Denise and Tony, fourteen months between Tony and me, and three years and eight months between JoAnn (Jo) and me.

My grandmother Anna was my dad's mother whom we called Ma-Ma. Most folks called her Miss Anna. She had been a midwife for many years in the county where we lived in North Carolina. Ma-Ma was a very important part of our family.

The four of us children played well together most of the time. Mommy insisted that we share and be kind to each other, and we did. But we had our moments when togetherness was not our goal. Did I fail to mention I was mischievous? Add that to my introduction. Still it seems there was always a parent, grandparent, or adult around most of the time when the idea to do mischief stirred.

Mommy did not have to worry about a babysitter or proper nourishment. Ma-Ma was there and with a snack ready for our eager appetites. It may have been apple dumplings, sugar cookies, or other pastries made with fruit. Whatever it was, it was tasty, even those big homemade biscuits with homemade pear preserves. That was good eating; but, she was much more than a great cook. Ma-Ma was strong and sure. She helped raise her grandchildren as she believed. It was a different time back then, and we did not have the freedom of expression with regard to saying whatever thought erupted. Respect towards our elders was high on their list. Grandparents were priceless.

My mom's parents were James and Agnus. Most folks called my grandfather Alfred and my grandmother Pearl. Both used their middle names in their community. I heard business associates refer to my granddad as James, but I never heard anyone call Grandmother Agnus. I didn't know that name until the end of her life many years later. James Alfred and Pearl were well-known and respected in their community where practically everyone knew everyone else.

I cannot remember my grandmothers meeting someone in the counties who was not connected with someone else in the county. There were no unwelcome strangers to the community. If they met someone for the first time, through a quick conversation they discovered the parents, grandparents, aunts, uncles, or some of the kinfolk that connected that visitor to the area. They asked, "Who are your folks?" With a simple connecting of family dots, they could give a synopsis of the family, and made the person feel welcome to the community. It was like watching a welcoming committee or area ambassador, and they were not the only ones to do this.

It was a part of country living. Everyone kind of watched out for everyone else; and knowing the families connected everyone to everyone else. It was just good old southern hospitality. This complimented the delicious foods gracing the kitchen tables in their homes.

Many times I found trouble trying to use adult lingo, butting in their conversations, and trying to act like them. The grown-ups were not having it; after all, a child had his place. I remember once when Ma-Ma had the church ladies over to the house for something and they were sitting in the living room talking. The ladies were separated from the children playing in the adjacent room. Whatever the subject, it brought much laughter. When I heard them laughing, I got up off the floor where I was playing, and walked to the open-faced doorway to hear the conversation. I stood outside the room looking in, and when they laughed, so did I although I did not know why. One lady said something and then another, and shortly after, the laughter followed. I laughed again and again.

No one noticed me standing there. Soon after, another of the ladies began to speak, and I yelled *shut-up*. It did not come out of my mouth the way I thought it would be spoken. It was loud and abrasive. My grandmother rushed over to me and popped my hands and mouth and ushered me out of sight with an explanation of why my behavior was inappropriate as silence fell in the room with everyone's turned head in my direction.

My feelings were hurt. I cried and wanted my mom knowing she would understand and take my side and vindicate me somehow. Certainly she would tell Ma-Ma she was wrong. When Mommy arrived a few moments later, I rushed to her side and began spilling out my story. I explained that I listened to the door while the ladies talked and then walked in the room full of senior citizens and told them to shut-up. My mom looked shocked and popped me too explaining under no circumstances was that acceptable. I started to cry again. My mom silenced that commenting I owed my grandmother and the church ladies an apology. "What were you thinking, Jackie?" she asked. I was just trying to be like them and talk like them. It just did not sound the same coming out of my mouth.

When I apologized, I explained to Ma-Ma how it was supposed to sound, and she told me I was still wrong. She reminded me that there is a different conversation for children speaking to children and children interacting with adults. The ladies agreed and did not seem to be angry with me. They seemed pleased to receive the apology or maybe pleased to share some wisdom. Either way their expressions were very different this time, so I was glad. They smiled at me as I walked out of the room this time. Later Denise and Tony told me how I had begged for an old fashion spanking and received just a little pop on the hand. I realized everyone was correct, and I hoped my mom would not mention it to my dad. She did not mention it, and I was thankful. Although my parents were married, my father was out of the home most of the time.

Both parents believed in structure. My siblings and I learned that it was much easier to follow the rules than to defy the natural order of things. We learned this, but we still did not always practice it even though we knew there were serious consequences.

My dad was a stern disciplinarian. If he promised a whipping, you got a whipping. You may actually receive it at the end of the week, but he remembered each time and I got it. Mommy did not delay carrying out the punishment. If she said you were going to get a spanking, you got it right then. It came swiftly. They were different yet definitely on the same page with discipline.

On the weekends sometimes as the entire family was gathered in the kitchen we sang while preparing breakfast and getting ready for church. Everybody sang gospel. The songs humbled us for a time. The lyrics and melodies just took us to a different place, a different mindset, and we enjoyed the feeling, the experience. Gospel music would do that for us. Honestly we sang about things we never talked about. It brought us together in a way that nothing else did.

The love of music was something my parents had in common, and they sounded terrific solo and great together. The songs were very personal, spiritual. They sang rhythm and blues too, but there were noticeable differences with the gospel tunes. There was a unique feeling. It was the joy. Ma-Ma sang her gospel songs and would hum a tune in a minute. She was not concerned about harmony or pitch, she just sang from her heart. That was Ma-Ma, and that was okay. She sang her songs as though no one else was in the room. Her attention was on her God, and it came from the heart. She didn't sing blues or rock and roll; only the gospel captured her heart in this season of her life.

Reaffirming his love of gospel music, my dad took the entire family to gospel concerts when the artists visited our area back in the late 1960's and early 1970's. We saw local artists as well as the renowned. It was exciting, though the adults always seemed to be in a hurry.

Once we arrived at the venue and sat as close as we could to the entertainment stage, the adults began to relax and enjoy the concerts too. We were allowed the freedom to sit, stand, clap, or however we wished to convey our enjoyment as long as we behaved appropriately. The adults glanced occasionally to check on our safety and make sure we were doing as we had been told earlier. We received our instructions before leaving the car. We knew how we had to behave in order to attend another outing. There would be no horsing around. We could not leave our area, we had to be respectful of others around us, and we had to watch out for each other.

It was unanimous, a fun time for all. The room echoed the sentiments of my parents and others having a great time. It was fantastic. The music was unbelievable with accompanying guitars and drums. I loved the sounds from the piano. I remember popping my fingers, jumping up and down, singing with the artists, clapping my hands, and just being overwhelmed by the music that sounded so good to me. I could feel the music in my chest. It was as though my whole body was responding to the sounds. I loved the feeling. After this delight, we slept on the way home. That was a bonus for the adults. We would start out talking about the experience and shortly afterwards, conversations dwindled, and sleep took us home. The next few days were full of conversations of what we saw, heard, and did.

The adults probably needed a quiet break from us. We could be a handful. Nevertheless, I liked being around older people, especially the elderly. They always had such good stories to tell, and they did not mind sharing their stories. Each of my grandparents was at least 60 years old when I was born. It was fun imagining them as younger people especially someone my age as they shared these fascinating glimpses into another time. They were great storytellers, I could see it. Ma-Ma's facial expressions changed as she turned back the clock talking about hard times and racial tension. The pain in her voice showed her mind drifted and placed her at the scene of some challenging times. It was the same for Granddaddy and Grandmother, my mom's parents. It was as though they felt those moments as they remembered. Life is funny that way. I loved to hear them tell it, even the sad stories. I listened as though I was watching a movie unfold before my eyes. They always left me wanting to hear more.

Grandmother was more interested in our present state rather than her past as she stressed education and was insistent with regard to the teaching profession. It was not a light-hearted matter to her. She was very serious about it. Education was her thing. When we mentioned other professions—after all Perry Mason was my favorite television personality—she pointed to teaching. She had great faith in the teachers of America and the work and skill required for the youth of tomorrow. She even wanted our games and play time to be productive. We just wanted to have fun and were often too loud for the indoors. We were hushed and directed to go outside to play and talk as loud as we wanted…outdoors. We did not mind because outdoor was so much freedom to play as we wished. So out we went gladly. Since they lived on a farm, we found many things to do to interest us. Grandmother tried to keep us on our best behavior even while we were out to play, but telling us not to get dirty did not prove obtainable many times. I guess it was possible, just not probable.

I was seven years old when she taught her grand girls etiquette for the young lady. She stressed posture, sitting correctly, speaking clearly, heads up and backs straight. She showed us how to sit with our legs crossed and the proper voice tones. Elbows off the table and no talking until the person speaking had completed his sentence. Waiting to speak was not only proper but also a respectful listening skill. There were no exceptions. Walking with books steadied on our heads, she corrected our posture. We caught on pretty quick, and she loved it. Though it seemed like a game to Denise, Jo, and me; it was not a game for my grandmother. She did not play games with us. Tony did not mind since he did not have to go through the same. He just wanted us to hurry so that we could come back outside to play with him.

Granddaddy was a farmer, and he impressed me; though he was small in stature, he was strong. His passion leaked out every day as he'd get up with purpose, determination, strong hands, and a ready mind for the job ahead. He was not easily distracted. I could barely pick up the corner of a bag of feed for the farm animals or the seed for the fields without someone helping me, but he could. He would sling a bag over his small shoulder and head for the tractor or head for the pigpen. He was a patient man, and a friendly guy. I understood why people liked him. His word was his bond. It was his philosophy and one of my mom's favorite slogans, so she taught it to her children. Also, she would tell us that we would be judged by the company we kept, so be a good person and pick good friends.

Mary, my mom's oldest sister and James Jr, her only brother, did not live far from the homestead. Some years earlier, they lived outside of the state of North Carolina, but now everyone was staying closer to my grandparents. The three—my aunt, uncle, and mom— frequently gathered at the homestead where their sister Leronis lived with their parents assisting with their needs.

My mom birthed the only grandchildren. Her sister Mary talked about adoption and foster parenting but stayed so busy that it never manifested. She was an elementary school teacher and quite busy in the community and church. She directed her affection towards the four of us. Surprisingly she did not want to be called aunt. We did so in the public environment because it was expected, but she preferred being called by her name, Mary. Sometimes we forgot to call her Aunt Mary around other adults outside the family. This caused some problems for us as the adults outside our family corrected us. After a while, we did not attempt to explain. We just added aunt to her name. It was easier, and the grown-ups did not accept our explanation anyway.

Aunt Mary was firm, kind, and serious about education too. Slang was not tolerated around her. The thing about having a teacher-aunt or aunt-teacher, she never took a break from teaching. She corrected us in the morning as well as at night. We were always learning. She did not like jokes about being ignorant. She did not have a sense of humor about that. Education was far too important to her. It was her passion and the story of her life. She wanted us to be excited about learning. She had great expectations and education would help make this happen.

My mom and dad were fortunate to have conventional relationships with their family. Even though my dad's father was not a part of our lives, the rest of his family was an intricate part. The youngest child in his family also, my dad was well loved by his family. My dad's siblings lived either in our county or nearby communities. Whenever we visited his sisters, Alice and Maggie, or his brothers Charlie and Kerry Lee, they enjoyed each other. We were always around kinfolk.

Dinner and church were not the only time my family gathered. The family shopped together. To buy groceries, we had a caravan of Mommy, Grandmother, Aunt Mary, Aunt Leronis, and the four children most of the time until I was about twelve years old. Grocery shopping was a family ritual. There were coupons and green stamps. These women went with a plan, a grocery list, and plenty of conversation. The women shopped together, the men did not. They were home or anyplace except with the women and children while we shopped. It probably seemed pretty peaceful to the men and liberating to the women. As for us kids, we did not care either way.

Shopping was not limited to groceries; the four of us kids trailed the adults as they walked from mall to mall, plaza to plaza, and one store after another. We tagged along on our best behavior most of the time. Usually we were well-behaved; however, we were kids, so sometimes not so well.

Boredom brought mayhem. Once in a department store Aunt Mary had given me her pocketbook to hold as she looked through racks of children's clothing with Mommy. It was heavy. I tried to give it back to my aunt, but she kept directing me to hold it a little longer. As time passed, my arms grew tired. I sat on what appeared to be the base of a mannequin stand to get relief. Looking up there was a lady mannequin standing tall above me wearing a long dress that touched the base of the stand slightly covering her feet. Denise, Tony, and Jo were playing quietly while I held the heavy handbag. Suddenly I had a great idea. I took the heavy pocketbook off my shoulder and put it underneath the long dress which covered the purse. You could not see it at all. My arm and shoulder felt much better. Now I could move about as freely as Denise, Tony, and Jo, and the pocketbook was safe. A load had been lifted off my shoulders, and I could play again. I was happy.

We continued to walk around the store, and I forgot about the pocketbook. I did not think of it again until Mommy and Aunt Mary were at the cash register attempting to pay for their items. They asked for the handbag, and I told them I did not have it. Searching themselves and the corners of their minds, they came back to me and asked if I had it at one time. I said yes. A sigh of relief came from them. "Where is it?" was the next question. "I put it underneath the long dress on the tall lady," I told them. "What lady," they asked with raised voices almost sounding like a choir. I tried to explain, but they began to panic and it started sounding a little bizarre while using the vernacular of a young child to a bunch of grown-ups, and the word mannequin would not come to mind. "The lady standing still with the long dress, I replied while mimicking her stance. She doesn't move," I explained.

It did not make sense to them at first as they envisioned a human being. Seconds later someone said, "The mannequin!" I nodded in agreement. Frantic we walked around the store trying to find the right one, and finally I saw her. "There she is!" I said as I pointed and ran towards her. "She's got your pocketbook!" Some shoppers turned to follow the excitement. I ran over to her, lifted the hem of her dress, and pulled out the big purse. They ran towards me glad of what was in my hands.

A huge sigh of relief came from all of them. Everyone was so glad to see the purse. They said they were scared it was lost. I was scared too. Aunt Mary said she had everything necessary in it, and by its weight, I believed her. When I pulled the purse from underneath the dress, my aunt quickly grabbed it almost embracing it before looking inside for her belongings. The purse was untouched. I think it went unnoticed by consumers and store staff. That was a blessing. We headed back to the cash register, and I felt like a hero even though I caused the problem in the first place. The conversation was about the hidden blessing instead of my mistake. I was glad.

Grown-ups seemed to be on a mission to keep us out of trouble, and we were on a mission to keep them busy. We were not looking for trouble, but things that seemed fun to us were not the least bit amusing to the adults. Before we left home to shop, visit friends and relatives, or any out-of-the-house activity, we had "the talk." The talk reminded us to be on our best behavior; no exceptions.

There were some basic rules. This was not friendly chatter; it was instructions. We were not to embarrass our parents or ourselves by word or deed. We could not touch anything we were not buying, and since we did not have money, we were to keep our hands down at our sides. We were not to talk loud or abruptly drawing attention to ourselves. Horseplay while outside the home was a no-no. We were not to beg anyone for anything. We were to get permission before receiving anything from adults, and we were never to talk to or take things from strangers. If our parents were not visible, we should politely decline things offered to us while speaking appropriately.

"The look" was another parenting tactic, and this expression was given by eye contact. It may have been a raised eyebrow, squinted eyes, wide opened eyes, or a sharp glance with a stern facial expression. The expression told the story of what could happen next if we did not refrain from what we were doing. Mommy gave "the look" and we paid attention to it quickly regaining our composure. She was not the only one who gave this look. It seemed everyone in our immediate family had taken this class and was well versed in conveying this facial expression. Apparently, other parents knew also as we noticed some of the other kids' behavior after the stare of their parents.

It was as though the grown-ups read our thoughts. New mischief could be on the horizon but cut off at the crossroad by the look. It said, "Don't even think about it. I'm watching you." We have backed down many times because we caught the look. It saved us when we were in danger of ignoring the guidelines of the talk. For some odd reason, when we were getting ready to do some things, we checked to see where the adults were located before proceeding. Even as a teenager, I remembered the look. When I was about to cross the line, and Mommy was nearby, I caught the look and closed my mouth or straightened up. It still worked.

Visits to Mommy's relatives in North Carolina were commonplace. She was extremely close to her cousins. Some lived in Gates County where we lived while others lived in nearby Perquimans, Camden, and Pasquotank counties. Some left the small town but returned often. Still others simply stayed in touch via telephone. Of course, there were disagreements, but the harmony was sweet. Nothing disbanded their cohesiveness. Some of her cousins were like sisters to her regardless to how far apart they lived. Those that lived in New York and other places did not allow distance to separate their affection.

When they came together, there was good old fashion fun. The grown-ups acted like little kids. They laughed as they spoke of old boyfriends, girlfriends, and silly things they used to do. They shared old stories and new ones. I think the grown-ups had more fun reminiscing about the good old days than we had laughing and playing with their children who were our ages. Everyone benefited from the visits. It was a family reunion whenever they came home. They did not wait for the official reunion. Mommy borrowed her dad's truck, loaded up the kids, and took us to visit.

There was so much laughter. Everyone was glad to be together again. The adults talked to the children. The atmosphere was charged with electricity of family camaraderie. Mommy had done some of the same things we were doing. She attempted some of the same aggravations and received some of the same punishments. She was like us. That thought was funny. It felt good to know she had made mistakes along the way and received spankings also. Mommy got a spanking. Mommy was mischievous. That was funny. Even as they laughed, we knew from our own experience that it was not funny when it happened. It took time to build humor. Mischief had cost them too. This reminded us that our parents were children.

Each of my parents visited his relatives. We visited each set of relatives with the respective parent. Daddy took us to visit his family at their homes quite often in the early years. We visited not only our aunts and uncles, but also cousins who reminisced. We had many first cousins on his side of the family, some our age while others were much older. All of Daddy's siblings were married and all had children except Uncle Kerry Lee.

We were always visiting family. I do not even think we called it a visit. We just stopped by and were welcomed. Mommy borrowed her dad's truck for her errands. She did not own a car at this time, and my dad drove his car. Family expected you to stop in, and they accommodated whenever you did.

Saturday was a good day for visits. It started in the late morning and continued to the evenings. We usually got a chance to watch a few cartoons before leaving home on our journeys. My dad and mom would gather us and go riding; sometimes the trip consisted of only one parent. If a few groceries were needed, they were purchased first with a quick return home, things put in their respective places, grab a snack, and start visiting family and friends. We played with our cousins while the grown-ups talked. Sometimes, we were in the same room with them, but we were in our own world. Others times we sat quietly on the sofas while the grown-ups talked. We understood being on good behavior. The talk and the look applied to family visits also. All rules applied.

Daddy grew up in Gates County, the same community where we lived. Aunt Maggie was his only sibling to live outside the county. She lived in nearby South Mills, North Carolina. Ma-Ma was devoted to all of her children and grandchildren though she lived with us. Family was family.

It seemed we could weather any storm as long as we had family. Occasionally we had colds and childhood diseases, nothing severe. Whenever we were sick, hurt, or bruised, there was a cure. We did not visit the doctors too often, but we had herbs, home remedies, and we had mothers. Mommy, Ma-Ma, and Grandmother were a powerful force. When the three of them united, whatever we had soon disappeared. There were antidotes for practically everything. They were always pitching preventive care. Put on your hat, wear a jacket, and stop jumping out of trees. It was sound advice.

I loved the outdoors. I did not want to wear dresses. They were too much trouble, and I had to keep them clean. That was a lot of work for an energetic rambunctious little girl. I usually followed instructions—the way Grandmother wanted us to walk, talk, sit, as well as other things —but I wanted to run, jump, and turn somersaults. Anytime I was in a dress, I felt caged. Of course, none of this talk was suitable for a little lady, but it was just right for the tomboy in me.

Sometimes we simply did the opposite of what we were told. One Sunday, the third Sunday of the month, we attended Mommy's church with her family. Daddy was not with us, neither was Ma-Ma. They did not go with us when we attended Mommy's church in the nearby Perquimans County which was about fifteen miles from our home. We did not return home directly; instead, we shared Sunday dinner with family and friends from the area. This particular Sunday's guest list would include granddaddy's pastor and family. They were scheduled to arrive at the house shortly after service allowing time for food and table preparations.

Mommy told us to sit on the front porch in either the white wooden rocking chairs or the green steel patio conversation chairs until they called us inside to eat dinner. The front porch was different from the back porch. It was a much larger area and divided into two seating compartments. One half of the porch enclosed with wire-net screening offered lounge chairs, two rocking chairs, and a table with fresh-cut flowers in a clear glass vase. The other portion of the porch was completely open giving more flexibility to those enjoying the luxury of the outdoors. It was not infringed by doors, windows, or screening. It provided three white rocking chairs, two green steel chairs, and two small tables which occasionally rested flowers. This is where we were supposed to sit until called for dinner. Though we could not leave the porch, this was almost as good as being outdoors on the grounds. It was unrestricted. For some reason, we felt the screened area was for grown-ups and special occasions, whereas the opened area surrendered to your own imaginations.

We were still dressed in our Sunday best while we sat in place. After a short time of waiting, we became bored. Tony started talking about climbing the trees just to the right of us. In the past, we played games in the trees. We could play games again if we were able to get off the porch. It sounded like so much fun. We decided we did not have to stay off the porch for a very long time; just jump off, run, play, and quickly return. It could happen so quickly that we would not have time to get dirty. Mommy did not have to know; we were convinced we could be very careful and not get dirty. This way everybody would be happy. As we talked, the anticipation grew. We talked about the possibilities, and suddenly as we glanced at each other, we ran and jumped off the porch running towards the trees with all of our might. Pretty dresses were swaying in the wind and a nice suit running with them. Not all of us ran though, only three.

Denise remained at her seat as she screamed to us that we could not play without getting dirty. Something would show up on the clothes, she said. We assured her she was wrong this time. This time we would be extra careful. We called for her, but she refused to come. We argued that we would not get in trouble if all of us climbed the trees, but she would not leave that porch. Now standing at the edge of the porch, she echoed a plea for our return. We motioned her to follow us, but she folded her arms and said no. We did not care. We played anyway. Soon enough we stopped asking her to relinquish her position. We talked to her from the trees and even made a game of her in her space and the tree climbers in our trees. Besides, we named her our lookout person to keep us out of trouble. We created fictional characters and the trees were people and places. The porch was Denise's house as she created her own fiction. Caught off guard while talking to us, Denise did not hear Mommy opening the door.

Furious at what she found, Mommy yelled for us to get down out of the trees instantly. Her expression was even more unpleasant as we slid down the trees with pine tree bark claiming snags and stains to our outfits. We could not get out of the trees fast enough or without damaging our Sunday clothes. Tony split his pants. They ripped as he tried to slide and jump out of the tree. The moments were getting worse. We looked a mess. I pressed my hands down the sides of my dress, and JoAnn followed the pattern trying to smooth out the damages. We became entangled in strings and pulled them for relief only to find out they were part of our dresses. Denise was in trouble too although her troubles were minor compared to ours. "We're sorry," we told her before, during, and after the disciplining. We tried to reassure her it would not happen again. She knew we were remorseful because we were caught in our mischief. She hurried the clean-up process and changed our clothes. We could not adequately explain how we attempted to stay clean and not ruin our clothes. Our words seemed useless. What an awful sight! The pastor, his family, and other guests were soon to arrive. Denise was silent as we walked back to the porch. We were silent also while Mommy pointed at each seat assignment.

Refreshed with moments to spare, we greeted the visitors as they arrived. They never knew the fiasco that had taken place moments earlier. The table was arrayed with elegance, and the four of us stood picture perfect nearby. Mommy had worked quickly with the three of us. A sigh of relief did not begin to tell the hidden story. It did not happen again. We continued to play in the trees but not in our Sunday best on Easter.

YOUTHFUL LEARNING

Television introduced the world to us. The people on television included depictions of the starving children in Africa. Americans were willing to help and established helplines so that telephone callers could offer financial support to feed the children. Some of those children were our age and younger when we first started noticing the program, and that was scary. Our parents reminded us how fortunate we were to have a home, food, and other things while those children were in need. We could not deny it; the evidence was before our eyes. We wanted to help also.

We offered our pennies to Mommy and Ma-Ma whenever the churches collected for the organization. We did not mind sharing and felt every little bit could help. We still did not want all of the food on our plates all of the time, especially our vegetables, but we ate them because of those children.

Everybody in our home enjoyed watching television at some point of the day or week. Ma-Ma had her favorite shows which included soap operas, The Big Valley, Rawhide, Bonanza, and she loved televangelist Oral Roberts. She watched those shows faithfully sometimes adding The Lawrence Welk Show. My mom added Perry Mason to the list. As far as my brother and sisters were concerned, Saturday mornings belonged to us after our baths and chores were done. That meant cartoons! Looney Tunes and Scooby Doo were the family favorites. Mommy's favorite cartoons were Dennis the Menace and Charlie Brown. We liked those too. We laughed as we saw similarities between cartoon characters and reality. We saw ourselves in them; we did not mind pointing it out and laughing about it. Reruns still made us laugh. The shows were funny.

There were not a lot of programs that the children of our house were permitted to watch, but some were acceptable. We sometimes watched wrestling and even a glimpse of boxing with our dad. My parents regularly watched the morning and evening news. Matter of fact, whenever the news was on, we could forget about any other program. News was priority. Sometimes the news reports were flattering, but it seemed more often the news reported the sad news.

At times, the news was scary. I was not supposed to be watching, but I did so quietly not to disturb the adults. I was only five years old when Dr. Martin Luther King, Jr was killed. I still remember the day I saw the report. It was horrific news, as though someone killed a member of my family. A chilling scream from Ma-Ma echoed the news as she yelled for my mom. Ma-Ma was in the kitchen standing in a visible path of the television in the next room. Mommy had gone to her bedroom for something before returning to the kitchen where the two were preparing dinner. She ran out of her bedroom where she found Ma-Ma trying to speak through her tears, but she was choked up. Seconds earlier she had been humming, laughing, and talking while making the biscuits, but suddenly she could barely speak. I stood up from my red rocking chair dropping my doll on the floor. They yelled for my silence. Mommy asked what happened. Ma-Ma stammered pointing to the television with tears drenching her cheeks, "Y-vonne, th-they killed him, they killed him! Lord, have mercy, Reverend King is dead!" Mommy cried out in shock and disbelief, "What? Oh, my God, they killed him! When?"

Again, I tried to find out what was going on, but they silenced me. My eyes turned to the television for answers since they were pointing in that direction. Simultaneously they turned and rushed near the television quieting each other so that they could hear the details. I listened for answers as they showed Dr. King. I saw him lying on the concrete floor outside his hotel room. I felt very sad for him.

Even though Dr. King had never been in our home, never met my family, he was yet a part of the family. My folks felt as though they were a part of his family. They stayed near the television for a long while. It was a miserable day. Preoccupied, the grown-ups did not explain what happened. I do not think they wanted to explain it or say it aloud anymore. I looked up at the wall where his framed picture hung. His picture and a picture of Jesus Christ were the only pictures of people other than our family members that hung on our wall. This meant that they were a part of our family too.

That evening, they told us what happened. A beloved man was dead. We asked questions because it did not make sense to us. They tried to explain in a way that would not scare us, but it was awful. In my mind while they explained I saw the news report. The scene with Dr. King lying on that floor kept flashing in my mind, and they could not explain that scene away. They did not realize the image in my mind; no one knew how I felt. I did not talk about it, but when the news appeared of Dr. King's funeral, I stayed near the television. I watched to figure out what was going on in the grown-up world that invaded my space. As the nation mourned, we mourned too. I did not watch the news for a very long time after that. It was too sad.

There seemed to be a change in the atmosphere, but it did not appear to be pleasant. There were noticeable tensions. The grown-ups seemed irritable. Conversations were full of discretion as we entered the room. Only occasional conversations affirmed their hidden feelings about the tragedy. We were silent because they instructed us that way, but we heard their pain.

Months passed, and it was time for me to attend first grade. Our schools integrated the next year; however, my first grade year witnessed segregation at T.S. Cooper Elementary School. It didn't seem different since the kids I played with and talked to on a regular basis were the same race. I was excited about the first day, but anxieties were present also. When we arrived at the school, I did not want to get off the school bus. No one knew because I did not complain, but I did not want to go inside the school building. I had mixed emotions about school, but it seemed the natural thing for children to do. From the catwalk through the opened doors, I kept moving towards the classroom. I wanted to be like Denise and Tony. They attended, the adults were happy about it, so now it was my turn.

I met my teacher, Mrs. Vee, prior to the first day of school, and she seemed nice, but I was still not thrilled about this all day adventure. With a little book bag in hand and Denise and Tony at my side, we walked towards my classroom. I wanted to find my place in class and sit down quickly and quietly. I noticed one of my friends in front of me walking towards the class. She was holding her mother's hand swinging it back and forth as they walked together. She was not smiling, but I knew she was okay. After all, her mom was with her. Disappointed with my predicament, I kept moving as Denise and Tony assured me that everything would be okay. Their classrooms were down the hall only a few doors away. I was still nervous as they ushered me to my seat and proceeded on their way to their classrooms.

Later that morning I saw Mommy through the viewing window of the classroom door. My heart started pounding with excitement. I called to my teacher, pointing at the door informing her that my mom had arrived. She greeted the teacher. They talked for a few minutes and then Mommy stopped by my desk to see if I were okay. I smiled and nodded assuring her that I was a big girl. She smiled stroking my cheek with her hand then cradling my chin and giving me a big smile. I knew she was pleased. Suddenly the challenges of getting to my classroom did not matter; the approval in her eyes assured me it had been worth it. I was officially a big girl like Denise. One day it would be JoAnn's turn, and I would walk her.

Although it was not lucrative, driving the school bus gave Mommy opportunity to stay in touch with our teachers and school activities. It was good to have her nearby most of the time. Periodically Mommy came to the school to check on our progress. It seemed quite often actually. She made a point of letting the teachers know they had her support. Our teachers and principals were quite pleased that she was so involved. I was not as thrilled years later as the early years.

I talked continuously in first grade back in the day when teachers spanked children. The teacher repeatedly asked me to stop talking, and I always stopped for a moment, but when she turned her attention away from me, I started talking again. I did not think about the repercussions of misbehaving. After all, I was not pushing or shoving, I was just talking...a lot. On this particular day, she said quiet down, and I did, but later continue to talk. She continued to repeat her request. Again I stopped talking only to start again. She called me to her desk. She gave a couple of licks on my bottom. She did not remove or lift my clothes, just tapped my dress. Embarrassed, I began to cry. She directed me to go and sit in my seat quietly.

Of all the days to check school progress, Mommy picked this day. I saw her at the end of the hall talking to my teacher during the break. I was glad to see her but suddenly afraid that my teacher may tell. This had the possibility of disaster. If Mommy found out I would not listen to my teacher, I would be in big trouble. I thought of what would happen if Mommy found out. Then I noticed they were laughing. Laughing? Mommy was not mad at all.

It was safe. The two were standing by the ice cream counter, and they were laughing. Ice cream! That sounded like a good idea. Since Mommy was smiling, everything had to be okay. With a big smile on my face, I walked down the corridor to the area where the two of them stood. I asked Mommy for ice cream money, and she gave it. I purchased the treat, said thank you, and started eating my ice cream. I was happy. I actually skipped until Mommy, and the teacher simultaneously corrected me.

Mrs. Vee called to me as I opened the ice cream top and peeled back the paper wrapping. At first I thought I was in trouble for skipping until she said, "Jackie, come and tell your mom about your day." Mommy smiled as she anticipated the response of great happenings. I explained what the teacher discussed to the best of my recollection. The teacher was precise. "Tell your mother about your behavior." I held my ice cream a little tighter than before in silence at first. I stammered, "I-I got in trouble for talking, Mommy." My mother looked at me and said, "You know better, Jackie." "Yes ma'am," I replied. Mrs. Vee said, "Tell your mother what happened after I kept asking you to be quiet and you continued to talk on several occasions." I said, "I got a spanking." Mommy gave me 'the look' and said we would talk about it when we got home. I happily said okay and skipped off with my ice cream. Thinking back, the skip is probably what messed me up.

Mommy knew the teacher very well, and she knew she would not abuse her authority on any of the children. The teacher called abruptly. "Jackie, come back here. Tell your mother what else happened." My mom asked what else could have possibly happened as she placed her hand on her hip. I said that I kept talking. My mother's countenance and posture changed sharply as she was aggravated at the news. I knew punishment was inevitable. Explanations could not save me now. Thank goodness I already had my ice cream in hand because I was not getting another treat for some time. I turned and put my head down and tried to speed-walk steadying my ice cream with both hands as I moved away from them. Relentlessly, Mrs. Vee called me back one last time. I thought if I kept moving I could get away from them. I wanted that more than anything else. The teacher continually spoke to me about the chatter, but now it was a problem.

There was a silence as I walked back to the two standing looking at me without a smile anywhere in sight. The teacher instructed me to tell my mom everything that happened. I tried to explain as I told her that I had not stopped talking as asked and was in trouble several times that day. "Really, Jackie? You would not stop talking when she told you to close your mouth over and over again?" Mommy said. With my head folded, I lifted it enough to respond in agreement. Her voice was poised just enough to demonstrate her disappointment as she spoke moving her lips but not her teeth. "And you've got the nerve to ask for ice cream. Give me that cone," she said as she took it from between my clutches. I started crying, and she told me to go back down the hall to my classroom, close my mouth, and have a seat, adding that I had better not give the teacher any more problems. She gave me a firm look. I owed an apology to the teacher. She asked why I felt deserving of ice cream. I said I did not know; I just wanted the ice cream. Another spanking was promised and to tell my dad.

I knew I was wrong even at that early age. I was very conscious of what I was doing. I was not mad about the ice cream; it was the least of my concerns. I was scared about the next spanking and my mom telling my dad. I was about to get a whipping for showing out at school. A tap with a ruler constituted a spanking at school, but I knew the real deal would occur at home. I remember thinking, why didn't I just shut up. Why did I keep talking? It never happened again. I talked, but not enough to get in big trouble with Mrs. Vee. I learned when enough was enough.

I saw Denise and Tony at school. At times, they were in the hall with their classmates and teacher lined up for an activity of sorts. Other times I saw them as I walked pass their classrooms peeping inside attempting to say hello unnoticed by their teacher or mine. They would sneak a wave but not speak out. They were careful not to disturb their class or teacher. I called their names out; it made them smile and sometimes shake their heads. The smiles made it worth it. Sometimes their teachers detected my presence and waved. That made me smile.

The next year integration swept in. Changes began with the school we attended. There was another school in the city, the Sunbury Elementary School. It was a large two-story building whereas T.S.

Cooper Elementary School was a one-story building. The school buses emptied all children in our neighborhood attending public schools from the first to the third grade into that school. Now there were Black and White children attending instead of Whites only. The teachers were both races. Still it did not seem like a big deal to me, but for many people it was a very big deal. I did not grasp the concept of hatred; I did not understand the hostility. The children seemed okay. The building was overwhelming, but the students were just kids like me, just different shades. My family talked about the adjustments my sister, brother, and I may experience during this critical and necessary change. Jo still had a few years before undergoing this ordeal, and they were hopeful the kinks would be gone before she started school.

The bottom line was a good education. Mommy said to display our best behavior, play nice, and behave friendly towards all of the children. She expected this no matter where we were and school was no exception. Dad said to do our work, pay attention to the teacher, and remember our home training. I remembered 'the talk.' Before the end of the first grade I had settled in and learned to be a little less chatty and more productive.

I saw my old friends and made new ones. Children did not seem to have the same hang-ups as adults. We played and learned together. When the challenge of racial differences occurred, the teachers were there to make sure everyone respected everyone else.

The evening discussions at home were about school. One question had prompted another question before the answer spilled out. My parents wanted to make sure everything was okay and that we were fairly treated. Tony and I were at the same school, but Denise stayed at T.S. Cooper School since she was in the fourth grade. All of us had stories about similarities and differences, but no one was harmed in any way. The teachers were like Mrs. Vee. They enjoyed teaching us.

Every year on the first day of school, Mommy visited our classrooms. Even though Tony was a boy, he did not get away without a visit. Once JoAnn reached school age, Mommy did the same thing for her also. As she met homeroom teachers, she always informed them of her support. It was her way of letting us know that she had set expectations from us. I suggested that she did not have to do this anymore, but she assured me that she knew what she was doing. Other parents visited also. Teachers expected and welcomed the visits from the parents.

As a habit, I talked to Mommy when she arrived home after work. I cannot remember how the visits started, whether she asked me to come to her room or I just ventured in. When there was nothing going on, there was still plenty to discuss. Everything was something to talk about. Some days she seemed to need a few more minutes to relax before the chats. In retrospect, she was probably taking a breather before the little chatter-bug came to her room to talk her ears off, but she never complained. I stood at the door and watched to see what she was doing. I was careful to determine when it was my time so that she would give me her undivided attention. I would not bother her too long. And if the door was closed, there were no visit to her room. That was private time. I figured that out.

Her usual bedroom etiquette did not allow anyone to sit on a neatly dressed bed. Making the bed was a ritual done as soon as we got out of it. There was no crawling back in the bed or sleeping late even though JoAnn always tried. This particular day I had somehow forgotten protocol while visiting in her bedroom and had stretched out across her bed to talk to her. She did not mention it; she just listened. I watched her eyes. Whenever I talked to people, I looked directly into their eyes. Had her countenance alerted me of the error, the conversation would have ended. I do not remember what we talked about, but that the incident has been etched in my mind from that moment on. It became important to me. She did not chastise me for breaking this rule. Somehow it had been okay.

Mommy always said the bed was a place to sleep; it was not a chair, table, or trampoline. Sometimes I had been guilty of using it for all three. She was very particular about certain things. Sit in the chairs or on a stool she insisted, but not on the beds. We lived in a small, three bedroom house, and she wanted it to stay at its very best, and chairs were provided in the bedroom. Those beds had to last a long time. We couldn't afford to break them again jumping up and down on them.

As I was leaving the room, I remembered that I had gotten off her bed leaving the covers jumbled from my hand raveling. I saw the messy bed. I put my hand to my mouth, and my heart pounded rapidly. I thought of past chastisement for jumping on the bed, bouncing up and down turning flips, and those pillow fights. I knew I was in trouble. I could feel my eyelids rising high as though trying to reach the top of my forehead for answers to the question I feared being asked.

Mommy followed behind me. I anticipated a warning, punishment or something, and at the very least questions about why I had been thoughtless. Whatever the consequences, I was scared. Taking a few giants steps, she turned to face me. I do not remember breathing, but I am sure I did it ever so quietly. She said everything was okay. It did not register in my brain at first. Even after she repeated it a couple of times, I did not know how to respond still unsure of my good fortune. She turned back to her room and walked over to the bed and smoothed out the crinkles. Even though it brought a sigh of relief, I walked out of the room quickly fearing she may change her mind. No spanking, no reprimand, just a smile. I wondered about my good fortune but did not ask any questions just glad at the outcome. From that moment, something changed in the relationship. I knew if I needed a break she would give it. I was more important than the rule, and that felt special. My life became an open book to her from that time.

Denise usually tried to keep us out of trouble but sometimes she was in the thick of it with us or leading the pack. She seemed to have the same fascination with hair as me. We used our towels to help lengthen our hair to the long flowing length we preferred with the likeness of our television family during our inside-the-house-play-time. We did not bother to change the style of our hair since we had the towels. We just put them on top of our heads and got on with play time. Jo joined in as we played grown-ups dressing in our Sunday clothes and putting on three pairs of Mommy's shoes that we discussed could never bear scars or scrapes else we would lose these instruments of beauty forever.

We were extra careful with the shoes. We continued the same story line each time we played, just adding more adventure to our lives. Denise was a movie star, Jo was the truck driver, and I was the lawyer. We were all princesses of course later adding husbands and children. It was our fantasy after all. We picked areas of our bedroom for our homes inside the castle and Tony joined us as a prince discussing his travels all over the world with his fake sword dangling from his side. The time was limited as we were only permitted inside playing if it were raining outside. It was so much fun as Denise played the organ in our bedroom singing her new hit songs. We laughed as we all played the organ, sang, and danced. We could not play so the noise was horrendous, but we pretended we played just hitting keys and occasionally hitting a good note. Nevertheless, we had to keep the noise down and not disturb Ma-Ma. Otherwise she came to the room to quiet us, and if this happened we had to stop playing and change back into our everyday clothes. This would mean the remainder of the rainy day would be spent quietly reading books instead of finishing playtime. Reading usually followed playtime.

Denise did the unthinkable; she cut her hair to create bangs. She cut the bangs very short. She did not plan to cut them so short. She was talking while she cut it and made a big mistake. She tried to curl her hair so that the adults would not notice, but it was pretty short. She tried to readjust her hairstyle to make it unnoticeable. Finally, she decided to stay out of the eyesight of the adults. This only lasted for a short while as Mommy was going to comb her hair on the next day, Sunday, for church. Mommy called Jo first. Once completed, she started on my hair leaving Denise last. We were thinking, hoping, and praying that maybe she would be distracted and forget her or not notice a significant chunk of missing hair in the very front of Denise's head. She was talking to Ma-Ma while she arranged the hairstyles. Hopefully that would be enough to get a quick hairdo and hide the mishap. Finally, it was time to comb Denise's hair.

Mommy started removing the bands that positioned the hair so nicely hiding the mistake. She unbraided the hair and began brushing the soft hair. She continued to talk with Ma-Ma. We watched her fingers. As she moved to the front of Denise' hair attempting to grab the hair as she brushed and talked, her hand glided across not gripping any hair. Silence swept through the room as we saw her hand positioned. She stopped talking and attempted a closer look. Immediately Denise tried to salvage the moment and explain her motivation behind the haircut as she received her reminder that hair cutting was not left to the children's discretion. This was one reprimand she endured alone. We had no part in it, but we felt really sorry for her as she cried through her chastisement.

I learned from that ordeal, I would not cut my hair. I had picture day at school some time later, and I wanted to wear my hair in a different style than the one my mom selected for the picture. We were too young to style our own hair. Mommy took care of that for us without our input. I thought the hairdo of braids that my mom displayed was too much like a little girl and I was too old for it at nine, but I could not say that out loud. Once I arrived at school, I changed my hair in the bathroom creating a bang, a ponytail with a ribbon hanging freely, and the bottom hair free of a ponytail. I liked this look. When the photographer said smile, I did so graciously forgetting the picture would represent the changes made to my hair. I hoped Mommy would forget and think the pictures were so pretty that it did not matter. The pictures arrived; she instantly knew I changed my hair. I tried to deny it at first, but the dishonesty was obvious and I admitted it. A spanking reminded me of the importance of the truth. She did buy the pictures.

Something started happening with my parents. There was a noticeable change in our home, but not to the unsuspecting outside world. The kids played, and the grown-ups dealt with their issues, which sometimes invaded our space. We did not discuss such things with them.

At the end of the day after a nice warm bath came pajamas and prayers, but we did not mention those issues in prayer to be overheard by the grown-ups. Knelt at our bedside in our favorite pajamas, my siblings and I prayed in unison a bedtime prayer. Tony joined the girls as we knelt together even though we slept in separate rooms. All of us prayed together for years. Sometimes it sounded as though we were singing because we said the same prayer night after night. It was mandatory each night before getting into bed.

Quietness filled the house as the adults listened. From the other rooms, they heard us clearly and harmoniously. A flick of the light switch and a crawl into our respective places invited more conversation before finally falling asleep. With our individual pillows, we slept at the head of the bed with JoAnn in the middle. Sometimes Tony slept at the foot of the bed until later when awaken by Mommy and taken to the sofa in the family room and properly tucked in his bed.

When summertime arrived I did not want to sleep. It was never easy to fall asleep in the summer. One night when sleep was far from my mind and the light from the sunshine still present, I was not ready for bed but already in bed for the night. I was sure I could have played for a few more hours instead of going to bed. We did not have the option of staying up as late as we wanted. Awake long after the bedtime prayer, it just seemed far too early to be in bed. I wanted to watch the Perry Mason show, which aired at our bedtime. I could hear it on the television in the next room. I do not know why I loved the show so dearly, but I did. Nevertheless in the summer I did not watch it for a few years because of my age and the time it aired on television. The introduction music was the signal to prepare for bed. I had a love/hate relationship with the theme music for the show.

Hearing the music increased my desire to see the show. I made up a song and sang it in an attempt to compel my mom to let me get out of bed. I sang while Perry Mason tried his case. Sometimes I sang while the show ended, and the music played. I sang each syllable lengthening the sound and singing it louder. I sang it so much that my siblings caught on, and all of us sang together. I sang trying to persuade her to rescind the order of bedtime. "Maa-my, Maa-ahh-my. Maa-my, Maa-ahh-my. Maa-my, Maa-ahh-my. Let me up. Please let me up. Maa-my, Maa-ahh-my. Maa-my, Maa-ahh-my." She did not respond immediately. She allowed the chant to go on for a few times while I stayed in bed. I was tired of singing it but did not want to give in.

Finally, Mommy required silence. She reminded me that bedtime was necessary, and my lullaby was not. She understood the purpose of the song while I tried to sing my way out of bed, but it was not working. She was not inspired. After some necessary prompting, I was willing to sleep and committed to not singing that song. I think everyone won that day. I was tired of singing; Mommy was tired of hearing it, and as my sisters and brother lying next to me was tired of it too. Now everyone could rest.

Everyone's bedtime was the same time even though there were six years between Denise and Jo. This was at a time when Denise was not ten years of age yet. We got up early and played most days outside after our chores were done. Summers were fun like that. We played school, stick ball and even invented games. When it was bedtime, it was not debatable; it was bedtime and prayers.

Daddy was not usually home when we went to bed during the summer nights. On this occasion, he arrived earlier. He agreed with Mommy that it was time for bed with one exception: Tony did not have the same bedtime. He could stay up a little longer. We asked if we could stay up longer. We received a resounding no. This was not a happy moment with the girls although we could not openly express it to our parents. We told Tony that we wanted him to choose to go to bed. He refused and said it was not his fault our dad made that decision. It was just for one night he suggested rather smugly. We did not like the idea, not even for a night.

We were preparing for bed angry while Tony was in the living room watching television. It was bedtime. Denise, Jo and I agreed to leave Daddy out of our prayers for the night. We could skip his name in the prayer list, pause, and move on to the next person since he wanted Tony to stay up and we had to go to bed. We figured he would want back in our prayers and let us stay up too. We began to pray aloud.

At the end of the prayer, we said, "God bless Mommy, noticeable pause in Daddy's space without his name, God bless Ma-Ma, God bless Grandmother and Granddaddy, God bless our family, God bless the hungry children, God bless everybody, and God bless me. Amen." Mommy yelled to us. "You left out your dad. You'd better add him back in your prayers." She suggested trying to warn us to prevent the chastisement. Too late, Daddy was in the room with a spanking for all three of us. He said it was not right to dismiss someone because they had not done as you wanted. It was wrong to leave him out of our prayers because we were angry with him or to use our prayers to manipulate others.

While receiving our spanking we yelled, "God bless Daddy. Please bless Daddy," adding him. Tony said when he heard us praying he thought it was a bad idea. He knew we would get in trouble. By morning, we wanted to find out what Tony saw on television. After the spanking, we fell asleep, so we did not listen to see how long he stayed up. He said it was not a long time because he was usually in bed, so he fell asleep anyway. I believed God forgave us, Daddy too.

After this time, my prayers changed a bit. I prayed twice at bedtime, once with siblings and then alone in bed when I turned away from my bed-buddies to fall asleep. I started praying about things I wanted changed (not just my bedtime hour). After these prayers, I said goodnight, snuggled under the covers, and fell asleep. There was a great comfort knowing God was listening to me at night when I prayed. I realized pouting was not going to cause my parents to change their minds about our bedtime or anything else. They did not give in to games like that. I grew up a little that summer. Finally, at peace I went to sleep at bedtime.

Summers were not long enough. We visited relatives, and there was no talk of bedtime. Mommy's cousins were a great source of laughter. It always sounded like a party.

All of us liked visiting the farm. Granddaddy was the farmer. He was so dedicated that he made it look easy. With sweat on his brow as he returned home from work, he never complained in front of us. He was the height of my mother but worked as though size had nothing to do with accomplishment. Whether he was in town handling business matters or on the farm, his enthusiasm impressed me. A strong man, he would throw the bags of seed, fertilizer, and feed over his shoulder as though they were lightweight. We could not pick them up. He worked Monday through Friday and many Saturdays, but not on Sunday. Since the Hickory Cross was one area he commonly farmed at the homestead, he was home at lunchtime.

Granddaddy was genuinely a very nice man. He had four grandkids and he made each feel important. He always had a smile for us, and that meant a lot to me for some reason. He pinched a cheek or gave a pat on the back, and it made me feel tall. I guess it was because he did not get to see us in mischief mode, so he was always positive around us. It was good stuff.

One summer afternoon while we visited our grandparents, Denise, Tony, and I decided to help in the fields. We wanted to help with the farming because it was our granddad's passion. Tony rode back to the house on the tractor with Granddaddy sometimes, and that appeared to be a lot of fun. Even though the oldest of us was only eleven years old, we were confident that we could help with the farm work. We really wanted to help. We decided to work an entire week rising before the sun. We wanted to work until evening.

It was all set. Mommy talked to Granddaddy, and he approved it with the exception of JoAnn. He said she was too young for the fields, but she could help Grandmother have something cool to drink when we arrived home from the Hickory at lunchtime.

That first day started with such excitement. We stayed with our grandparents the night before so that we could rise early. Bedtime was not an issue as we anticipated the next morning. At the hint of dawn, we were up, beds made, and dressed. No one had to wake us. Exhilaration was our alarm clock.

There was a cool breeze that morning. Aunt Leronis cooked a hot breakfast. Mommy drove as we rode in the back of the Ford pickup truck feeling the coolness of the morning breeze in our faces. We continued to breathe in that cool fresh morning air as we rode for a short distance. As soon as the truck stopped, we hopped off the back jumping from the tailgate. We started running through the field kicking up dirt and twirling our arms intoxicated with the idea playing all day. It was awesome. We decided to take off our shoes and just have some fun running and playing in the huge field. The soil was dark, rich, and cool underneath our feet.

We threw dirt at each other and played for about five long and intense minutes. That was the amount of time it took our mom to talk to Granddaddy and noticed us in the field. She ran down the row waving her hands high in the air to get our attention insisting we had to stop playing, or it would ruin the hard work done the previous day. She seemed upset as she spoke of the time and effort used planting seeds in the soil where we were trampling. I wondered what she wanted us to do. I did not want to use the hoe to chop weeds yet; my thoughts had been playing in the fields. Maybe we thought we might get around to it when we got tired of playing. I wondered if Granddaddy knew about Mommy's new instructions, but I was not about to ask.

The fun stopped as suddenly as it had begun. Instead, we worked the first row together receiving directions from Mommy. Next we were responsible for working entire rows individually. The rows seemed to stretch from one end of the state to the other end. From where I stood

I could not see the end of the rows or the house that sat upon a hill across the street.

While we worked, the heat replaced the cool of the morning. We reminded each other that we asked Mommy, even begged her, to let us work in the field with our grandfather. We realized we were nuts! We wanted to back out of the deal, but they would not let us. We tried to explain we wanted to sword fight with the hoes, not chop with them. Initially we wanted to help Granddaddy. After we had thought about the fun we could have in the fields, we lost focus. We apologized. "Now can we play," we asked. Mommy simply pointed to the rows to work.

We did not get to work with Granddaddy. He was in the field, but he was on the tractor, the fun mobile while we were on the ground with hoe in hand. It seemed as if we were miles from him. We did not talk to him; we could not even see him because the fields were so large and the hills sloped. Each of us had a mission and a hoe. We were not happy about either.

At last, end of the day approached. We had our Granddaddy back. He rallied us to tell us how proud he was of us and how well we worked. He said he caught a glimpse of us working hard and deliberate—although he did not phrase it that way, it meant the same thing—and thanked us for our diligence. He promised to pay us something for our labor if we kept working with such vigor. He said though this was our first time working so purposefully for extended hours, it did not look like it. By the time he finished talking to us, we were excited again. Mommy said we should not focus on the money, but we did anyway. Now we had an incentive, payment. We talked about all of the toys we planned to buy with our money. Each of us named at least four or five items. We agreed to work in the fields for the rest of the week as promised. We asked Mommy to take us to the fields even earlier the next day. She agreed and was glad to find us excited about the field again.

At the end of the week, Granddaddy called us together and told us it was payday. He said we had worked equally hard so he would pay all of us the same wage. Captivated by his words we stood at the doorway of the back porch that led into the kitchen of his house as we awaited the rewards for our labor. Even though Jo did not go into the fields, he advised her help with lunch all week was worth payment also. Of course, the young JoAnn had done very little, but he wanted to reward her. The speech ended. We stood in a line and waited eagerly to receive our pay. He smiled summoning us one at a time so that he could tell us how much he appreciated our commitment. He was brief. Then he issued the money. With Mommy at his side and a big smile on her face, he put the money in our hands.

He gave each of us eighty-five cents. In 1972, eighty-five cents could buy some great treats, but little that we planned to buy with our wages. We thanked him, walked outside the house, and stood in the back yard under the umbrella tree. Finally, I said it, "Eighty-five cents, is that all we get?" We looked at one another and opened our hands to the palms where the payment of our toil rested. Imprints traced the coins in my hand from the tightness of my grip. I wanted $35.00. I do not know why, but that's the amount I quoted over and over as I bragged about what I planned to buy. It had a nice ring to it. We were disappointed, especially me, but we decided right there under the huge umbrella tree not to tell anyone how we felt about this. We made a pact that it would be our secret. And it was until now.

We decided not to tell Mommy either. We said we would not beg to work in the fields anymore, but the subject of payment was a closed issue. "Nobody says nothing," we repeated. Suddenly we started laughing at ourselves. We were up early mornings and rushed out to the fields for eighty-five cents. We could not stop laughing. Apparently we worked eighty-five cents worth.

Surprisingly it did not matter anymore and we could not stop laughing. Mommy ran to the back porch because of the noise. From the window pane, she saw us laughing. She opened the screen door and asked what happened. We were holding our stomachs and laughing jumping up and down and falling to the ground in tears. Finally, she just waved her hand, smiled, and went back inside.

We had shown ourselves faithful and dependable, and Granddaddy said he wanted us on his team next summer also. We gave him a big smile and turned to each other to a wide-eye affirmation this was not going to happen. We did not want to do this again. It was fun for him, but not us. We would help, but no more volunteering for early mornings and late evenings.

Being a good child sometimes was hard work. Some days it was obvious that we worked at it, other days we failed miserably. We tried to motivate, but sometimes mischief fooled us into thinking it looked better when we wanted the forbidden. It did not feel better when the truth was revealed, and the culprits received the just rewards. Laughing at each other while in trouble meant double trouble for everyone, so we just had to hope for the best for our fallen comrades.

The thing about mischief was you never knew when it would show up. Mommy was lying on her bed one afternoon. She had not been feeling well that Saturday. This meant we would not visit relatives or friends. We would stay home and play. However, we were looking forward to the visits. She just did not feel up to it. We waited outside her door sitting on the floor hoping she would change her mind. We tiptoed to her door and peeked inside as she slept. Tony was the first brave soldier to go and check, and then each of us girls peaked. Her closed eyes only frustrated us as we wanted to go. We started complaining about grown-ups. We sat there having this deep and meaningful discussion outside her opened door bedroom. We tipped back inside her room repeatedly verifying she was still asleep. Exiting her room and nodding to the other, we rejoined outside the door to complain a little more about the changes to the plan. We actually tipped inside the room and leaned in over the bed to make sure her eyes were closed before returning to the gang. With the go-ahead sign, the nod, we continued our discussion.

We talked about raising our children differently without rules and discipline. The grown-ups were mean. Our kids would get lots of treats whenever they wanted them and lots of toys. They could stay up at night to watch television especially shows like Perry Mason. We discussed how we thought grown-ups were mean a lot, especially when they told us it hurt them more than it hurt us to punish and spank us. We could not figure that one out. We talked too much.

Mommy was still asleep through all of that. Finally, we wondered about her since she never slept during the day, not even a leisure catnap. We hoped she was all right. Now really concerned we decided to check on her. We got up off the floor outside her door and walked to her bed to look at her sleep so sound. When we got to the bedside motioning to step quietly, she sat up erect in bed and said, "Every closed eye ain't sleep." She nearly scared us to death.

We screamed and ran out of her room. She laughed and called us back. Our eyes bulged, and mouths were still opened. Not knowing what to do next, we said nothing. Our eyes glued to her posture noticed that she sat erectly. It was the kind of thing you saw in a scary movie.

"Just remember every closed eye ain't sleep when you start talking about folks. You know better than that stuff you said. Don't say anything you are not prepared to say twice and don't say stuff that's going to hurt other people's feelings. Did you want me to hear that and do you even believe what you were saying out there?" she said pointing to the hallway. We knew what she meant and shook our heads with a no. I could not even remember all that was said but I knew I did not mean to hurt her feelings calling her selfish for being sick on our play day.

We were ashamed. We preferred a spanking or punishment if it meant Mommy would forget the things she heard us say right outside her door. Instead this time the shame of our words was our spanking, and it worked. For the rest of the day, we apologized. The next day we apologized more. She assured us that all was forgiven, but we wanted it forgotten also.

Our parents could not watch us every moment of every day, but they counted on the support of the neighborhood. People helped each other in our small community. It just worked that way. Whether the storeowner, school janitor, lunchroom worker, or the usher at church, everybody seemed to know everyone and was willing to help guide the children on behalf of the parents. The parents expected and welcomed their help. Neighbors kept the children in line. My parents did not get mad if our neighbors corrected us. Matter-of-fact, it was their charge if we misbehaved. Adults in the community also watched for our safety. If they found us in error, it was their job to put us back on the right track. If something happened to cause a phone call to my parents, we were in big trouble. Gates County was not the only watchful neighborhood; other neighborhoods were this way too. When we visited my mom's hometown of Perquimans County, we received the same reception. It was a community service. You did not have to ask them, it was the expected and acceptable thing to do. The villages or communities helped raise and nurture the children. We knew it. It surpassed the relative pool.

We knew our neighbors. Being a part of a community was a great work. People were congenial. They shared conversation, jokes, laughter, and tears. When someone was sick, others stopped by with meals and a smile to help the family. Especially at harvest time, people stopped by our home giving fruits and vegetables. We did likewise when Granddaddy harvested his crops. We shared with others. Everybody had a little something. Some had more than others, but everybody had something. If we were stuck in the mud, we pulled each other out. The community was essential. We remembered them in our prayers.

I remember one year Mommy told us that we were giving toys away for Christmas. That idea was okay since I figured we bought things to give away. Then she said to pick some of our toys to give. Confused at first I asked if she wanted us to give old toys we were no longer using. Even those were semi-important. Some things were easy to share; foods were available for all those who wanted some. Toys were in a different category. Mommy talked about the importance of giving and sharing. I understood but felt I should have the choice of what I wanted to give and share. Denise, Tony, and Jo felt the same way. Others had shared things with us...and now we could give something back. When put in those terms, we could not disagree.

Mommy insisted we take some time to decide which of our favorite gently used toys to give away. We went to our room and decided to give three toys each and items of clothing. I am not sure where she took them. I remembered when we talked about it, we decided one item was not enough. At first giving away one of my favorite toys was more than enough, but Mommy had a way of explaining why giving was necessary. We freely gave two more toys each. She said each of us could contribute something to the well-being of others, and we had a responsibility to care for our family. It was not our concern to point a finger at one who was ignoring his responsibilities; our job was to do what we learned as the right thing. It was simple.

During the daytime, family and neighbors cared for children if the parents worked. We learned not to be afraid of neighbors, the elderly, ailing, or handicap. There may be some physical challenges sometimes;

we just had to offer a helping hand. We grew up visiting the sick and bereaved. Mommy insisted people needed physical comfort during their healing process. When someone died, the comfort had to be a call, card, or visits to encourage the family through their sad times. This also meant we attended funerals of people I did not know. Mommy knew them and explained this was a part of the farewell process for loved ones. We had to support.

Our community offered the same. When my mom's school bus was stuck in the mud in our own yard, one of our neighbors came to the rescue on more than one occasion. He never charged for time or services. He just helped where he saw the need. After heavy downpours, our yard flooded with water continually. As it drained off, large potholes remained in the driveway. The yard always required some additional soil or a load of rocks. After a bad storm as we repaired the yard a neighbor may come along and help as we spread out the soil or rocks. We did not request it, but we appreciated the help. Once when our lawnmower was broke, a neighbor came to the rescue cutting the grass for us with his lawn mower. He and his wife stopped by and talked with Mommy first. She shared with them that our mower was broken and having come prepared to do the work, the man walked to the back gate of his truck, let down the tailgate, and pulled his mower down. He let the ladies continue to talk. Mommy thanked them for their kindness and said Tony could cut the grass if he allowed the use of the mower but he insisted that his mower was finicky. He mowed while the ladies motioned us to walk the yard in search of debris that should be removed to protect the mower blade. After a while, the ladies went inside the house as the children stayed outside gathering the sticks out of the way of the mower. We had kind and genuine neighbors. I remember that day as if it were yesterday.

Church was the community, and the community was the church. Two Sundays a month we attended my dad's church in Sunbury; once a month we attended my mom's church in Belvidere, and we visited other family churches during the rest of the month. There were different denominations and counties, but all in the family. Many people in one county knew the people in the other nearby counties. My brother, sisters, and I sang in both youth church choirs, ushered at both churches, and participated in the outreach activities. My mom believed in the church fellowship. The different denominations did not hinder that.

Dad's church was also Ma-Ma's church, St. Paul Missionary Baptist Church. He sang in the choir in his early years. When he stopped attending for a while, he still insisted we accompany Ma-Ma whenever Mommy did not attend with us. Ma-Ma was 65 years old when I was born, but she was very active like a much younger woman. We rode the church van as she reminded us of her expectations from us. When she exited the van, she sat in the church section with the elderly ladies enjoying her church services. We did not sit with her, but we acted as though we were right beside her most of the time.

Mommy's church carried her maiden name. It was her family church, Winslow Grove African Methodist Episcopal Zion (A.M.E.Z.) Church. She sang in their choir and in a couple of other choirs. Singing was one of her passions. Aunt Leronis ushered while Granddaddy sang in the choir. Uncle Jr sang on occasion too. Aunt Mary was the church secretary. There were lots of other members. The family simply worked in the ministry. Grandmother belonged to one of the other churches in her community, but also attended with her family.

Sunday mornings were ritualistic like preparing for school. I focused on the day ahead knowing I would see friends and family regardless of the church we attended. It was all good.

Listening to the preachers held my attention some times; other times it was the joy of singing and seeing friends that caused my happiness. When we socialized too much, a reprimand followed.

As young children, we had to sit near my mom or close relatives for the church services, but as we aged we were allowed to sit with friends. Too much chatter beckoned an usher to give the sign to be quiet. That was a no-no. When the usher stopped by my row and directed attention towards us, it assured a reprimand at home. If Mommy saw us and just gave the look, that shut everything down. I simply got up and sat beside Mommy. That way my trouble ended right there, and she was pleased. But she was not always looking at us. I know I mentioned the social aspects of the church, but even as a child, it was more than that for me. I was not always paying attention to the ministers, but sometimes I heard them and their words resounded in my heart. I was deeply touched, and it changed the way I thought about certain things for a while, sometimes forever. I believed what I heard about God's love. For some reason, it made me feel good. I did not understand, but I knew I felt good about that love. I wanted to be a better person. Still the mischief in me won in my inward struggles at times.

Baptized at nine years old, I made the request at first because Denise and Tony were going to the mourners' bench—a place of repentance, renewal, and rebirth—to give their hand to the preacher, heart to Jesus, and request baptism. I saw them get up and move forward as the pastor of the Baptist church gave the invitation. I got up and walked to the front. Mommy nodded that it was okay. I heard the preacher talk about Jesus. Listening intently now I heard words about an outward sign of an inward relationship with Jesus Christ. It sounded peaceful and relatable. Unsure of all he explained, I was going to ask him for clarification in front of all those people, but one of the ushers hushed me. The more he talked, the better I felt. I started to understand as I listened. I was glad for the invitation and the trip to the front of the church. I asked Mommy questions when we got home, and she was glad to answer. The water baptism happened days later. We could not stop talking about it for a while. Considered too young since she was only five at the time, Jo watched on. She joined Mommy's church five years later.

Jo was the youngest but seldom excluded. Usually she was in the mix of whatever happened even though she was not supposed to participate. She tried to keep up with us, and most of the time she did. If she was excluded, Mommy explained that it was not her time yet to be the active participant, but her time was coming. She reminded her it was important to wait, observe, and learn so that when her opportunity arrived, she would be ready. She found a way to include her in the discussion if simply to remind her to cheer for her siblings.

Family outings included everyone in our home although Ma-Ma seldom went with us. We liked the family trips to Nags Head and Kill Devil Hills, North Carolina for summer visits. We left home early in the mornings with sand pails and shovels for the handy work ahead. The drive was not that long, but an hour drive was long enough in a car with four children all under the age of twelve on the back seat. The

Carolina sun and sand felt so good. The sand just flowed through our fingers until dust residue settled in our palms. A gentle breeze kept us satisfied as we anticipated and welcomed it. Everyone played and laughed together.

Permitted to take off our sandals, we walked barefoot in the sand. We had to remember the location of our shoes, but it was worth remembering as long as we could run and play without them. It was exhilarating running up and down the sand dunes, seeing others riding dune buggies and having fun like us. It was just one day for two summers, but each visit seemed longer than a day as we played the entire time patiently building sand castles or whatever activity we made up. We built the castles, marveled at them, called our parents to witness our handiwork, and then fell on top of them to demolish them before starting again.

Food was not a priority for this trip. We brought food and drinks. Sandwiches satisfied the stomachs, but the sand satisfied our souls. It was all about the playtime, sheer entertainment.

There was no fussing as sand covered us from head to toe. Mommy told us to try to keep it out of our hair, but considering that every turn brought more and more sand, it was tolerated as we concluded a dirty and dusty day. We cleaned up before getting back in Daddy's car.

We talked about our adventures at the end of the day, but the drive home always proved longer than our conversations. Tired, ready for a bath, and waiting to collapse in our beds caused the drive to be a quiet one. We fell asleep offering our dad the privilege of driving in silence. The next few days were always full of conversations about the trip. It was always a great day.

PUBERTY TO MATURITY

In the sixth grade, I started writing in a diary. Mommy knew and allowed that degree of privacy. I started writing because of Denise. She loved writing poems, and I found that I did too. We had a knack for it. We wrote of all occasions sometimes making it a game. Then she told me about a diary. She said in her diary were private thoughts that she did not want to share with anyone. It became her sounding board of honesty without worrying about offending anyone or saying the right thing all of the time. It was like a friend. She had many friends, but this was much more personal. It was a great idea even though I had many friends also, and I had Mommy. Still this seemed unique, so we gave our diaries names. Mommy agreed to write was liberating, but insisted against isolation. It was okay to write, but I had to remember there were real people to talk to about things. I understood what she was saying. I told Denise what she said and dropped the idea of naming my diary, but continued to write.

I wrote about being a pre-teen, friends and puberty. When I was really happy or sad, I wrote. Family life was the subject quite a bit at the start. A lot of energy was given to my quiet thoughts about my parent's feuding. It was just easier to write things down that were not going to be discussed with them. It allowed my expression whether rational or silly. When I made sense of it, I told my mom some things. She said it was not silly when I was trying to understand. She encouraged me to stay a girl for as long as possible. I started to think that maybe she did not understand what I was saying. While it was true that she had been my age, I was sure it was so long ago that she had forgotten. This generation was different from the previous one.

My diary had no comment. I think that is why my mom was concerned. I started to see boys differently. All of a sudden the stuff Grandmother had taught about walking, talking, and sitting did not seem like a bad thing or a waste of time. It had become useful and I noted that in the diary. At first it seemed as my mom was trying to scare me with the ideas of growing up too fast, the danger of improper conduct with boys, and the problems that could occur. She said she was just realistic about the danger of the body over mind instead of mind over body.

Whether we kept a diary or not was of no consequence to Tony. Writing was not his idea of fun, but he did not discourage it. Building model cars and engines, drawing characters and scenic pictures were his passion; and he was talented. He drew in the mornings before school and on the weekends. It seemed as though he drew all of the time. Even during the cartoon shows; he drew what he saw. Many times he drew while we talked. He was an artist. When he had extra money he spent it on the cars. He also liked building things with sticks. That did not cost a thing, just time and energy. He was fine without an audience as he did his thing, but the writing was not it.

Mommy was always watching us. She knew me. Once I started talking about something, I was going to say exactly how I felt good or bad. I think she may have wanted to pull her hair out or maybe mine as she listened but she did not. She assured me that although feelings were real, I had some control over my feelings, and I had the power to determine what was necessary to me. She said my thoughts did not control me, I controlled them. She insisted that I place less emphasis on boys and more energy on school work. This warranted more school checks and grade scrutiny. She checked almost everything stressing purpose and obligations.

Much time was spent maintaining a healthy childhood. Summoned for conversations, it was not hard to chat when she offered a topic. I liked talking with her even when we did not agree. She listened. A lot of times we laughed about things that had appeared very serious. It was just good conversation as Mommy brought clarity. Tony and Denise joined the talks at times, and we laughed about our zany lives. Jo listened and shared too. This made serious topics approachable. Mommy listened as we joked about mishaps. Often right in the middle of the laughter she offered correction on what we should do the next time. It just did not sound like correction, but it was. When we started to get out of the line, she resumed her authority and nipped it, reminding us that our mother was still in the room. Glimpses of our day with friends, relationships, and school were discussed anytime.

I never read Denise's diary, and she never read mine as far as I am aware. JoAnn was a different story. Jo always tried to peep inside or over my shoulder. Sometimes she wanted to play when I wanted to write. It seemed to her I was always writing, but I was not. I enjoyed it though. This was a little frustrating to her as she had to share her play partner with a book. She wanted to know what I was writing and sometimes I shared; other times I stopped writing and played for a while. When I refused to play, she went away, but she was never happy to go. Usually when I finished, I hid the book in my drawer, under the bed or in the closet, but not this day.

This particular morning I wrote a comment before going to school. When finished I placed the diary on the dresser, grabbed my books and headed outside to wait for the school bus. Jo was already outside but had to go in for something and returned to wait for the bus with me. Evidently while she was in the room she picked up the diary and placed it in her book bag. At the end of the day, I realized she had it.

I was seventh grade, and Jo was in fourth grade. We were on the same bus while Denise and Tony were on the junior high/high school bus. We were headed home. While talking to some of my friends, I noticed quite a few students gathered to the back of the bus and were laughing. For an instance, I wondered what had everyone's attention but did not give it much thought. As they quieted, I heard some of my thoughts read aloud. Writing for almost a year now, I was comfortable saying whatever I wanted in my diary comments. I heard my words, jumped up, ran to the back of the bus grabbing the diary and Jo as everybody enjoyed a good laugh at my expense. Embarrassed and angry, I really wanted to disappear. I knew I was in trouble.

The real conflict came at home when my mom found out what happened. The bus driver was one of our neighbors. She called my mom with a report of the incident. Instead of JoAnn getting stern chastisement—which is what I hoped—I got the much needed correction. "She violated my privacy!" I attempted a forceful comment, not allowing my voice to elevate too much. I was embarrassed that my personal thoughts had escaped the diary and found their way to someone else's lips. I was ashamed of being so honest in my writings. The fight with my sister seemed to take center stage. My mother said JoAnn did not need whipping. I was wrong for hitting my sister while the bus driver was trying to get us home safely. Mommy spoke of different things that could have happened while I explained about my diary being taken from home, and private thoughts handled all day out of my domain.

There was no excuse for endangering everyone. With that as the focal, I realized I handled it wrong. We were practically home, but I had to stop Jo. There was no acceptable excuse. Standing before my mom I kept emphasizing my privacy. "You are twelve years old, Jackie! What was so serious, so much that you had to fight your sister? Don't say it again," my mom fired back at me. I could not win. Embarrassed still, I let it go. I had to apologize to my sister, the bus driver, and my mom. Jo apologized to me and then Mommy corrected her for invading my privacy. Jo said it was supposed to be a joke, but she had not really figured it out. After this ordeal, I hid the diary, and she did not read it again, or at least I never heard about it.

By now our grandfather was in his eighties and his doctor felt it would be more beneficial health-wise if he stopped farming and relaxed. He had been a diabetic since I was a little girl, but it did not keep him from farming. He had a terrible time with arthritis, and a new condition had been diagnosed. Granddaddy refused this notion for quite some time before finally agreeing to stay off the tractor and out of the fields. It was not an easy decision. Farming was not his occupation; it was his life. Nevertheless he finally agreed with the doctor. We saw him quite often, and although he had stopped farming, he was still kind. It did not seem strange to see him without the tractor since it was right after the harvest season.

One evening at home after dinner Granddaddy returned from the bathroom headed for his chair in the den when he collapsed to the floor never to regain consciousness. He died that evening. My family was devastated. The family rallied to support one another. I was glad I had friends and school to keep my mind occupied. He was not a young man, but he was Granddaddy.

His death really took a toll on Mommy. He was her rock. It was already a very stressful time in her marriage. Things seemed to be falling apart, and I was writing all of the time. I loved my grandfather; all of his grandchildren loved and admired him. This was a very sad time for my family and us grandkids. His death was a terrible shock. The loss was overwhelming. My mom tried to help us, but we knew she was in tremendous pain. We were struggling.

A month before seventh grade ended, the superintendent permitted a tour of the junior high school since we would attend in the fall. We loaded onto buses while the principal allowed us to unload the buses and roam about the premises of the junior high school seeing the teachers and students we would interact with the next school term. Tony was already there and sought me out. When he found me, we walked around as he guided me through the halls and school yard. He introduced his friends. He already knew all of my old friends. I needed this change.

Mommy was glad to talk about something different as she had many conversations with her family concerning Granddaddy and his business matters. People came with condolences and inquiries about the farm equipment. As for the grandkids, we stayed out of the way while we shared with each other memories of fun, laughter, and how he came to our rescue so many times.

We seemed to be talking at our kitchen table a lot. The same day I toured the junior high school, Denise toured the high school. She was excited. Next year would be Tony's freshman year and last year at the junior high school. Jo would also change schools to attend the fifth grade. It was a busy time for all. The junior high school contained eighth and ninth graders only. It was different from other community schools. We liked the idea of being at a school with only two grades before going to high school for only three years. It was unique. Anyway, Mommy promised her school visits would continue to help us transition with all of the new changes.

When we changed schools we developed a fondness for the telephone, even more than the previous use. This caused telephone rules. Daddy restricted us if the grades on our report cards declined from A's and B's. Mommy restricted us if there were incomplete chores or if we stayed on the phone too long. Ma-Ma wanted to know the parents of every caller especially the boys. The bottom line was simple. The adults saw the phone as a distraction. There would be no talking, giggling, and having fun on the telephone without obeying house rules first.

I developed anger issues—not because of the telephone. I did not realize my opinion of life was changing, and it was frustrating. Mommy sensed it. She started saying things like, "What's going on, Jackie? I didn't raise you to act like that. What's going on with you? You know better." At thirteen, it was probably puberty kicking in too. Our home life changed, and I hated the tension. Our dad was out of the home most of the time, and when he was there arguments were constant. All of us were trying to act as though nothing was happening, which only made things worse.

Talking on the phone became a battle between the Brown girls. Everyone except Tony wanted to use the phone at the same time, even Jo. Sometimes my privileges were suspended. Somewhat embarrassed I explained that I could not talk because… and gave the reason. This was part of my dad's incentive to do better by admitting our faults to the caller. When on punishment, I told my friends at school not to call me. I explained my predicament.

Ma-Ma insisted that at our present age, all boys needed jobs. Tony had one. She was a spry seventy-eight year old—though she did not look or act like a woman entering four score—she kept me on my toes. She had many memories of a time when boys, regardless of their ages, worked to help support their families. She asked if each teenage boy had a job especially during the summer. When one of the boys admitted he was not working, he needed to get off the phone, get busy, and get a job. He should help his family and prepare for manhood. She was serious about that. "Lazy boys make lazy men," she said. "And no man wants a lazy woman either." I just wanted to talk on the phone. I was not thinking about adulthood. Ma-Ma insisted it was thinking about me.

Mom said, "Don't try to be grown. You will grow up soon enough. Don't get caught in something you ain't ready for. Don't let your body tell you who you are. You tell your body who you are. Don't give mixed signals and don't give off the wrong signals. It ain't cute, and it can get you in a lot of trouble." She was relentless. I assured her I was listening. I think they saw the telephone as a gateway to inappropriate behavior because we wanted to talk so badly, and once we started, we did not want to get off the phone. Tony refused to get absorbed in phone calls. We were glad that he was not interested. That was one less person to negotiate.

Problems kept surfacing in my parent's marriage, not simple ones. The children may have heard the discussions but were not permitted to comment or speak of it outside the home. What happened in our house stayed in our house. That was the family motto back then. Some issues seemed to fade away while others lingered. Avoidance was a momentary solution. Music was not a remedy though previously it had been in hard times. No more Sunday morning sing-alongs echoed from the kitchen. The conversations lessened to awkwardness. There was not even a hint of pretense. Somewhere along the way they reached the point of no return. We needed him, but the gulf between them was enlarging. He made choices that did not include us while deciding which path to take. Again we could not talk about it with the adults since we were just children. We wanted everyone to be happy again.

A family break-up is not easy for the children. Tensions thrived. We leaned on each other respectfully understanding we were not to discuss it outside the home. "What happens in our house stays in our house." Ma-Ma offered help, but she was in an awkward position. We lived the event as though taking part in a tragic play. It was already written, casted, and performed.

In the past at the homestead my mom would have been in the den with her dad discussing such matters. He usually sat in his favorite lounge chair while she sat on the sofa directly in front of him. Slightly chewing a toothpick he always stopped chewing to offer sound advice. She would walk away confidently and relieved. No longer was his arm available to lean on. In retrospect, I am sure my dad leaned on his family as well since they were very close.

Several months later my parents' marriage officially ended. I was thirteen. I wanted the fighting to stop, and peace in our home. I wanted everything to be okay. We experienced so much pain with our grandfather's death; and now the death of a marriage. Mommy grieved for her dad for a long time. I was angry at life. Too much was going wrong. I could not figure out how to make this work and no one was talking with me about it anyway. I sounded off to Mommy, not at her. She tried to comfort me, but I really just wanted to be angry. I was confused. Finally, I backed off in silence before crossing the line, and gave her privacy. I did not want to be disrespectful. She had enough to manage. She did not need an irrational teenage daughter.

Everyone had his own way of dealing with grief. Denise, Tony, Jo, and I shared our thoughts about our grandfather and our parents with each other. We talked about what we overheard as well as what we thought was true. We did not share with the grown-ups because they insisted certain matters should not be discussed with children. But with us, there were no limitations or unapproachable topics. We understood the grown-ups did not understand.

Mommy worked through her issues sometimes in the soil as she planted, watered, and manicured her flowers. They were beautiful. She pampered the indoor and outdoor plants even talking to them gently as though they needed her words to grow. We joked about it at first, but it seemed to be a sensitive matter, so we stopped. She sang and played music for them, and every plant responded. It worked; therefore, the house and yard were beautiful. We helped a little, but it was more her project than ours. We offered a hand and sometimes my mom allowed the help, but she seemed to have a rhythm of her own.

The barrier between parent and child did not allow me to tell my parents what I thought of their problems. Respect kept me in my place. Relationship tragedy was wearisome. One morning while our parents were in their bedroom talking, they decided to end their marriage. The four of us children hushed each other so that we could hear as we listened with ears pinned to the closet in the girl's bedroom. It was quiet. Actually, it was calmer than it had been in a very long time. They reached an impasse and decided their course of action. Leaving their room, the mood was calm. We quickly exited the back bedroom. They summoned us into the sitting room for a family talk. They were very direct. It was not a shock since we just heard the conversation through the closet as they discussed how to tell us the news. It was a very thoughtful discussion as they were concerned about our reactions. It was the first time I heard the children mentioned in their conversation, but now we were the center of their thought. The time for change had come, and they wanted us to be okay. Earlier, I was convinced that they were not thinking of us while they battled for a solution.

Anger was getting the best of me, and I did not know what to do with it. I certainly did not want to suppress it. Mommy wanted healthy conversations. I wanted to vent, explode, complain, but she said no. She tried the mature approach, but I did not want to act maturely. She insisted. I decided to write about it. My pen was getting constant usage as I dumped my frustrations onto paper. She said whether I understood what happened or not, I could not disrespect my parents. I was obligated to speak with respect. When I tried to sound off, Mommy snuffed it trying to help me process the change without losing myself. I was angry at the world. The other children were disappointed and angry, but I seemed enraged.

After my father had moved out, Ma-Ma did so as well a few months later. We saw her a lot at first as my mom often took us to Ma-Ma's new home to help us transition. We saw her at church too. I never thought Ma-Ma would be a part of the separation. She belonged to us, to me, and it did not seem fair to let her live alone after all these years of living with us. She was with us all of my life. I never knew a time when she did not live with us except when she visited her other children.

The issues with my parents kept the two families estranged at first. We still loved one another though folks had to pick sides as the line was drawn in the sand. I could see it in the eyes of family. They checked on us with phone calls and visits. We saw my mom's family slightly more than in the past, but my dad's family not as often. We continued to see my dad's family at church on Sunday and throughout the neighborhood. Aunt Alice always had a big hug and kiss for us. We did not see Aunt Maggie as often since she lived in a different city and attended a different church. When we did see her, she likewise offered great affection.

I realized while writing this book that I became a cynical girl. I changed my idea of marriage and things in general. In the past, there were times as a little girl I cried about things that hurt my feelings. Suddenly, I stopped crying. I became hardened. I did not realize the depth of the evolution until now. I began to suppress some feelings while becoming very vocal about other things.

I did not cry at sad movies. That may not sound odd, but my compassion was dwindling. Their pain did not stir me. I had pain of my own. I felt the loss my grandfather and absence of a father. I decided to be stern, strong-willed, and determined. I needed to be self-sufficient so that no one's opinion defined me. My mind was working overtime. Mommy and I talked less for a while; marriage was the subject she did not want to discuss. She just insisted I respect their decision as it was for the best at that time. I just remember feeling miserable for some time.

Later we started our talks again. By this time, I stopped being that angry. I had written until I guess I found peace or at least I found silence. My mom talked about the loss of her dad, but she still did not discuss the separation. She refused. I tried to pry, but she stopped me. Finally, she told me, "Jackie, you're a child. I'm the grown-up. Let me handle this. I know you mean well, but this is my problem." I felt it was mine too.

Mommy's family and friends helped her process her discontent. She talked to an older cousin too. Their constant calls and visits kept encouragement flowing. Her cousin had a way of making her laugh. She knew she could count on her cousin for advice as well as listen when she needed to talk. I assumed my dad talked likewise with his family and confidants to process this new path. I wondered.

It seemed my mom found her solace in music. She had her favorite songs, played them almost every day in the living room, and learned every word singing it along with the records. The stereo blasted. When she first started I headed in the room to ask her about it, but Denise caught my arm motioning me from the entrance of the room. She said that it was Mommy's time and to let her sing until she felt okay. Day after day the same routine followed. Finally, Denise was nowhere near, and time had passed; I walked in the room and sang with her handing her a large serving spoon to use as her microphone. She laughed as I pulled another one from behind my back using it as my microphone. Then we laughed, sang, and danced together. I felt better; the point was to check on her, but I really felt better. I think she did too.

Thinning out our closets was a chore. It seemed as though we were always holding on to something that we should have disposed of the year before. There were things kept for sentimental reasons. It was funny that in a year or two the sentiment wore off. Each year we pulled things out along with our memories only to put some of the items away for yet another year. Others we decided it was time to let go. We reminisced about why we kept the items before finally boxing them for the giveaway. Sometimes we could not believe we bought certain items or that we were so passionate about keeping it when it looked so ridiculous later. We laughed while we boxed. Mommy looked over the items to determine whether they were acceptable donations or trash. My favorite purple dress kept surviving the process though I had not worn it since I was four or five. It was preserved in packaging to keep it in good condition. It was adorable, and I wanted to save it, so I did. After all, it was purple.

Denise got her first summer job at fourteen. The next year Tony followed. Finally, it was my turn. The summer of my fourteenth birthday, I was excited to work. Each summer we worked for the manpower program for the next few years. Mommy allowed us to open savings accounts, but we were not allowed to spend the money frivolously. We helped each other and alleviated some of the household financial burden. I liked designer clothes but did not buy them. I spent wisely so that the money would last as long as possible, and I was okay with that decision.

The summer jobs provided money for other activities too. Mommy did not request any of our pay, so we bought our school supplies. We decided among ourselves to buy for each other, made lists of things we needed, wanted, and divided the lists between us. She approved of our idea. With the three of us working, we insisted on buying many of Jo's school clothes and supplies. Our mom was with us as we made the purchases at first. If we bought clothes in her absence, we showed her what we bought. She was pleased with each purchase and allowed individuality. It felt like a rite of passage. We thought we were good with money. Savings lasted until well after Christmas. She was proud of us and told us so over and over again. When our summer funds were depleted our hands were extended to her, but she did not complain.

If Tony had money and I did not, he shared with me. If JoAnn needed something and I had the money, I gave it. Denise always saved in case someone was in need. That was just the way it was. We looked out for each other. During the school year, Denise and I did not work. When Tony was sixteen, he started driving the school bus during the school year which kept a steady cash flow for him and us. When he got paid, he just shared with us. He did not give all of his money, but he shared and that was good enough to keep us satisfied. We did not ask a lot; after all, it was his pay not ours, and we understood. A little lasted a long time. I wanted to keep all of my earnings in the house in a shoe box, but Mommy insisted the bank was the best place.

We were growing up. Our responsibilities increased, and we were allowed to hang out with friends, but we still enjoyed visiting family. Whenever Mommy visited family we were glad to ride along. We liked visiting our Aunt Mary at her home. She lived city-life compared to our rural area. After chores, she drove us to the nearby mall and gave us a few dollars each to buy whatever we wanted within reason. This also gave us a chance to spend the money rewarded for getting A's and B's in school. If we received less, we were encouraged to do better. She did not suggest punishment for the C's, but there was no reward. With a challenging subject, she encouraged dedicated study time rather than simply homework. We had to do our homework.

It had been almost three years since Granddaddy died. We were finally adjusting to his absence when mom's oldest sister, Mary, became ill and passed after a brief illness. She was diagnosed with breast cancer a year earlier. I thought she had the perfect life before that time. But now I saw her pain and suffering. The medications brought little relief at times. She declined chemotherapy. I wondered how this could happen to someone so health-conscious about eating and exercise. It did not make sense to me. She was not a fitness guru, but she was seemingly in good health. All of a sudden everything changed with one diagnosis. I was thinking too much, but things did not make sense.

The summer before she died, I was 15 years old. I stayed in Elizabeth City with her to help as often as possible. Mommy insisted and told me that my aunt was ill, and it was serious. I never expected a life-threatening illness. I did overhear comments leading me to the thought that it was some sort of female condition. Finally, I overheard another conversation that mentioned cancer. I told my siblings as we discussed the seriousness. Still we figured somehow she would get better though it may take a few weeks or even the entire summer. Aunt Mary was always there for us, so we had to be there for her even though I had no idea what I may need to do.

She never complained in my presence. I could see the discomfort on her face, but when I asked how she felt, she always said that she was fine. She gave me a chore to take me out of her presence for a while. I wanted to help her, but she was more concerned with helping me.

She was a constant busy woman always on the telephone making sure that situations were as they should be and handling many papers and files. She later told me that she was getting her affairs in order and insurance papers accessible for her husband Uncle Richard so that he would be able to find anything he needed in her absence. I did not think her absence meant death. I figured if he needed to find something and she was not in the house, he would know how to go to the files and retrieve information. I never saw him go to the file cabinet for anything, yet she was busy making sure labels where legible and appropriately attached to the files. I helped with that. She instructed the way she wanted everything displayed. She was very methodical.

She had great strength most occasions, but a few times needed to read the Bible and relax during the day. This was a signal to me that something was terribly wrong because my family did not rest during the day. It was true for Mommy's entire immediate family. Once out of bed regardless to the age, there was no lying down unless they were ill. Before this time I never saw my aunt lay down except at bedtime after her house was cleaned, swept, and in proper order. By the end of that summer, she was gone. It was another painful loss for my family.

Six months after Aunt Mary's passing, Grandmother died. It was unexpected. She lay down at bedtime and did not wake up the next morning. She was not sick to my knowledge other than diabetes which she managed mostly for as long as I could remember. There were several instances where she had been hospitalized from this disease, but not in recent times. With both parents and their oldest sister gone in three years, my mom, her sister Leronis, and her brother James Jr received a lot of comfort from family and friends. They leaned on their faith to keep them grounded. Uncle Jr needed professional help coping. An elderly cousin who recently had been staying at my grandparents' home had a stroke and passed away two weeks after Grandmother's funeral. The losses seemed to happen too often. It was such a sad time.

Aunt Leronis was still at the homestead where she had assisted both of her parents. Her younger brother Jr lived next door. They tried to encourage him, but his struggle was even greater than they realized as he struggled with his sanity. He was institutionalized when he declined his medications as he started to feel much better. He said he felt he could manage without the pills, but he could not. When he stopped taking them, it caused him to spend much time in the mental facilities as they tried to help him adjust with life's heartaches and a chemical imbalance. It was a battle. We missed him.

My sisters, brother, and I became concerned about Mommy. It felt like things were really falling apart. Her immediate support network was vanishing. She was very close to her brother but could not seem to reach him. She drove to the hospital with her sister to visit him after obtaining permission from the hospital hoping to bring him home; however, many times it was a visit only. Her smiles were fewer and her laughter faint. I did not understand how she could keep it together and show concern about everybody around her, but she did. She had to do so with four children counting on her for their comfort. She said she did not have a choice. We wanted her happy, and she sought it for everyone else. She seemed to make it her mission. Meanwhile, her flowers in the yard were beautiful from all of the care she poured into them as she would venture outside to the yard to relax, hum, and sing. She allowed us to help talking us through what she wanted for the flowerbeds even though we understood it was her project, her therapy to keep things in balance.

We were glad Mommy had family and friends that were concerned about her well-being. It was not just her kids that noticed her countenance had fallen. She looked sad for a while, and others saw it too. We encouraged our mom to visit so that she could have a change of scenery and maybe get her hearty laugh back. Instead, she checked on Aunt Leronis and Uncle Jr, and stayed close to home making sure our needs were met. She talked to her sister daily, and they took trips to the institution to check on their brother as they rallied to support one another.

After a season of tears, she started to regain her groove. She sang a lot. She prayed and sang in the mornings, and that sounded so good to me. It made me smile as I realized a change taking place. When the tunes changed from somber to upbeat, I could tell she was recovering from her grief. She was not forgetting them, but she was processing the pain and moving forward. The people she had counted on the most for support and guidance her entire life were gone. It was truly over for my parents. Others were gone too, she had to learn to deal with it and live. She tried to keep it light-hearted, so we laughed about silly stuff; it took love and strength from those that knew her best to help during those lonely times. She prayed regularly. I was not sure what to do to make her smile, but I wanted it badly. Finally that day came; quietly smiling without force until her laughter gained its momentum and returned. A hearty laughter was back, and so was Mommy; what a great day! I know it did not take as long as it seemed because it seemed to take forever.

So much had changed in three years. Our childhood was disappearing before our eyes pushing us toward maturity, and we had no choice other than to go with it. We kids talked about everything. We talked about what we saw happening and what we did not see happening. We talked about what we wanted to see happen. We talked about the good old days as though we were a bunch of older folks reminiscing about the days gone by.

Some of the important family members were no longer in our everyday lives. We really missed them. Our dad and Ma-Ma had moved out of our house permanently. We no longer had Mommy's parents or our Aunt Mary. Uncle Jr did not stop by our house a couple of times a week. He was at the hospital far more than at his home. We visited the homestead quite often, but the atmosphere had changed. My Aunt

Leronis was still very busy even without her parents. The homestead looked different with less farming machinery on the premises and even fewer farm animals. The fields were still there, but our granddad was not on the tractor plowing them. The two huge grapevines were still there, but they lacked the attention they were getting when my grandmother made preserves and grape juices. The gigantic weeping willow tree, which spanned an eighth of the back yard, seemed lonely as the family meetings outside under the tree with glasses of fresh delicious ice tea had ceased. Things were very different. We remembered and longed for the times passed.

I was glad to have an outlet, my friends. After the summers, school truly was a blessing. Friends talk about anything, and we did. We talked about family issues if we wanted, but we talked about so much other irrelevant stuff to keep my mind preoccupied. We laughed about something and much about nothing. It was like being with my siblings far away from the adults with no chance of overhearing their conversations of change or reflections. That was a welcomed change. Friends were fun and funny, and we could laugh about whatever. We shared the good and the bad. I could count on them when I just needed to be a kid, just a light-hearted teenage girl. I was a teenager and wanted the respect that my 15 years carried, but more than that I needed laughter. My friends had their own personal lives too, but they really helped me stay grounded. We played, fought, and learned together, and I loved them, the girls as well as the boys. We matured together making mistakes and living through them. Denise, Tony, and Jo counted on their friends too. We were growing up. We needed school, friends, and everything that came with them.

OUTCLASSED

Tenth grade was no different from the previous school years. Mommy still made visits on the first day of school. When I tried to talk her out of it, she said it was settled and not up for discussion. I was no longer the excited little girl waiting for the face of her mother. I felt anxious. I was watching the doorways; after all, this was a high school, tenth through twelfth grades. By noon, there was still no sign of Mommy, so I figured she would wait another day. A sigh of relief eased out. I felt I had outgrown the first day visits anyway. As soon as I relaxed she walked through the door of my English class, introduced herself to the teacher, and assured her support. I smiled as though it mattered not that my mother was standing at the desk of my English teacher. School and home were different. I wanted them to stay separately. Each area had its place, and the two should never meet. First day of school was meeting day.

That did not stop me from trying to get out of an algebra class. I asked my mom to write a letter to drop a class because the course was too difficult. Concerned, she asked if the teacher knew I was really struggling. I assured her that although the school year had just started, I could tell I was over my head. All I needed was a note of release, and I could take an elective instead. She said okay. In retrospect she did not say she was going to sign the note, I assumed she would do it.

The next day she forgot to give the note. I planned to turn it in as soon as possible. While I sat in algebra class, my mom walked in and politely asked to speak with the teacher outside the classroom. She agreed. Upon introductions, the teacher motioned me to tag along with them. As we walked, I knew it was not going to turn out as I had hoped. I could feel it and just wanted the moment to pass. Mommy asked about my struggle. The teacher replied that my class work was fine. She suggested I chat less and work a little more; other than that, things were fine. The teacher asked was anything wrong, had she missed something. My mom apologized for the confusion and assured her I would settle in more quietly. Both shared that they were glad to meet each other and went their separate ways as I received a smile and look from my mom.

I remembered thinking, what is the big deal? It is only math! I wondered why she did not just write the note. I did not want to mention it later at home, but she did. Math was not a problem in the past. Matter of fact I was good at it. It was possible that I was stumped, anything was possible. My mom said that she was not naive, nor distracted. She was focused when it came to our studies. She would not permit an elective instead of the math class and waste time. She said, "You're going to school to learn, Jackie. If a class is hard, that's okay. That's why you go to school. But you're not going to waste time doing foolishness. What you said didn't make sense. Don't cause me to go out to school for a bunch of foolishness. Let this be your last time. Do you understand? Am I making myself clear?" I quickly responded, "Yes ma'am." She emphasized the last statements with the firm voice I knew well. She asked why I wasted her time; I said that my reason was dumb and apologized again. I just did not want to take the class. She said, "Well you're taking the class, and you'd better do good in it too, or I will go back out there and you know I will." I agreed and proceeded to finish washing the dishes wanting to disappear down the sink with the water. I felt awful about the whole ordeal. It was a lie about nothing. I just wanted a free block of time.

At age sixteen, I was confident and curious; confident that I had the answers and curious to see if my answers were correct. Mommy applauded self-confidence and discouraged arrogance assuring me there was always more to learn. She stressed good grades and best behavior. She assured me fun should not be at someone else's expense. There was strength in kindness. I understood what she was saying but did not always want to abide by her beliefs.

By now I learned not to tell Mommy everything about my teenage relationships with boys. There was no sense in causing her ears to explode. I wanted to keep our relationship, and she was not a girlfriend though she felt like it many times. Even though I spoke freely with her and loved to talk with her, I learned what to share. She was mom, but I loved telling her what happened in my day. I could not resist it. She seemed so interested, and we laughed at the funny and dumb things I did. It did not feel parental. She knew I was not giving her every detail, but enough to give her a picture of what was going on. We laughed a lot. She knew dating was fun and social, nothing serious for me yet as I share that relationship stuff too—kind of.

Then Phillip appeared. He was different. I was sixteen and still talked with Mommy about boyfriends, friends, and whatever. When I started talking about him often, Mommy noticed something unusual happening. She said that the talks were different about this boy. She was right; it really was different this time. She knew by the things I shared. Right away I wanted her to meet him. He had been a friend of Tony's since eighth grade. He was an athlete, and a cute one. He had become one of my friends.

Tony always gave me the run down on the guys I liked. He was protective. He told me about their reputations and how he felt about them. He told me that guys talked about the girls they dated, wanted to date, and the ones they did not date. I respected his opinion. I knew girls talked about guys, so I was glad that he was there to warn me when I was swooning over appearance. Tony liked Phillip though. He gave me the run down on him too, and he gave him the thumb up.

My friends told Phillip that I had a nice mom, but teenage friends can set each other up sometimes. Therefore, he was not sure what to expect. There was a dance, the Sophomore Ball, and I wanted to attend with him. This could not happen without introducing him to my mom first. She was serious about that. I needed the two to meet and like each other.

Phillip met Mommy. She was sitting on the front porch relaxing when he drove up. I was so excited to see his car and know this was the day of the great encounter. Mommy told me to calm down and not appear that excited. I was not jumping up and down, or anything like that, but she could see the anticipation in my face as I smiled. He exited the car and walked to the front porch steps. I made the introductions.

He greeted her with a very pleasant smile and a handshake as he waited for the invitation to sit. She knew he was waiting and delayed it while she joked with him. They seemed comfortable with each other. They continued to joke as they talked. Things were looking pretty good. I wanted Phillip to leave so that I could hear what she thought of him.

Finally, he drove away. I followed when she left the front porch to enter the house. She looked over her shoulder and smiled as she continued to walk not uttering a word. I broke the silence. "So Mommy, what do you think? How do you like him? Talk to me." I said. She laughed as she replied that he was nice looking and seemed like a well-mannered young man. Somebody raised him to be very respectful, she said. He dressed nicely removing his cap as he entered the porch. She loved his sense of humor, and he seemed a little nervous. I started trying to explain when she cut me off. "No, I like that," she said, "It means he has respect for grown folks." From that day, he could visit. She liked him.

Phillip never blew the horn at my house to summon me to the car. He parked the car, came inside the house, greeted my mom and anyone else in the house, asked for me, and assured my mom teasingly that we would be back home after curfew. He came inside the house one day with a rose in his hand. I thought it was for me, but to my surprise, it was not. It was for Mommy. He said some quaint little phrase when he gave it to her. She smiled and thanked him. She smelled it, looked closely at it, and said, "Phil isn't this one of my roses?" He laughed and said yes. I looked at him because her flowers were her passion. While I looked on, I was sure he had blown it. Mommy laughed. He told her that he knew the kind of flowers she liked by the kind of flowers she planted. He was giving her something that he knew she had to love. She laughed, gave him a look, and shook her head advising him not to break her rose bushes.

One night Phillip was supposed to stop by my house and pick me up around 9:00 p.m. That was actually kind of late. Normally he visited much earlier in the day or evening, and if we were leaving, it would happen prior to nine. He knew the house rules about dating because I shared that information very early in our relationship. There could be no confusion. I had to leave the house before 9:00 p.m. He was permitted to visit with me at my home, but if we planned to leave to meet with friends, we could not leave the house after 9:00 p.m. For some reason, he was late and pushing the clock. I started to get a little anxious. Finally, he called to say he was visiting his cousin at his Grandma Hattie's house and would be at my home shortly. He had lost track of time, unfortunately but was sure he could beat the clock.

By the time Phillip actually arrived at my house, it was 9:05 p.m. At this point, he did something he had never done before with me. He blew the horn a few short strokes for me to hurry out the door. I heard it and tried to run out of the house grabbing my jacket and purse with a quick acknowledgement of my departure, but Mommy called me back. I hoped she had not seen the clock but was going to say something about him blowing the horn. When that was not the quick topic of discussion, I knew what was certain to come. Phillip was not early enough, and I was not quick enough to get away before the clock spilled the beans. My mom knew I was watching the clock. The conversation began, "I know you are not going out of this house after 9:00 p.m.," she said. "It's just after nine," I replied. She said I had not listened to my own voice, so she asked me to repeat it once more. I did, and she stopped me in the middle of the sentence reminding me that from my lips I acknowledged it was past the time. She said, "Its af-ter nine. You are not leaving this house after nine, Jackie. You know the rule. It didn't change."

Taking a deep breath, I stopped trying to defend my point. I could not win the battle. I certainly did not want to end up punished because I did not know when to stop talking. Seconds later she said, "Tell Phillip he can come in and visit with you for a while." I smiled, kissed her on the cheek, and ran outside to tell him. He entered the house apologizing for blowing the horn and arriving late. She accepted his apology.

He did not seem too disappointed about staying in that night. Instead, we sat and talked. We walked outside and sat on the swinging loveseat to talk under the moon and stars. He seemed to talk about things that I had not heard other guys discuss or show interest. If you asked him now, he would probably say that I talked more, but he took me to the moon. Actually we talked about the moon, stars, constellations, and what we wanted out of life. There was no dancing that night, but the evening was not wasted. I learned about him; he was not embarrassed to talk intelligently. I was love-struck.

I told Mommy about some of our conversation. She said she could tell that he had ambitions; he wanted to make something of himself. She said his kindness was only a glimpse into his character. She credited his family for establishing good values. She did not mind if I spent time with him or his family.

I enjoyed time with Phillip's family. There was mutual respect, and they were like my family. When Tony dropped me off at Phillip's house, he stopped in for a few minutes to say hello to Phillip's dad Mike or mom Eugenia (Jean), who was much like my mom. Phillip's mom did not meet strangers and had a conversation for everyone she met just like Mommy. If we were going someplace and my sisters were tagging along, they did not mind a visit with his mom. She welcomed all of us. Phillip's mom reminded me so much of my mother that it was uncanny. They seldom got angry and did not stay angry for very long. They had a love for people seeing the best in them or at least the potential to be good regardless to their actions. They looked right passed the foolishness. It irritated me occasionally because I saw the foolishness. I did not see the good in everybody. Some folks just seemed mean. These two moms said there was a reason for that. They thought way too deeply about humanity for me. I just knew what I saw and heard while they were always explaining that there was more. I did not want to be that deep and thought-provoked at the time. They said life was not surface. It was layered. Anybody could do something bad, but the intent may be to do a good deed. That was way too much credit given to people who did not care what these ladies thought. I called it wasted time, smiled as they talked, not even defending my point of view, reassuring myself that I saw the clearer picture. They were too nice. After all, I was the teenager, and that said it all.

One Saturday as we headed to the roller skating rink, Tony drove as Denise, and I tagged along. Phillip and some of our friends were there. We had a great time. When it was time to go home I left with Phillip since he had driven also and was planning to go directly to my house.

Both vehicles left and arrived at our home at the same time. We exited the cars and went inside.

My mom was inside. She asked if we had a good time and we responded yes. We returned earlier than expected, still full of energy from the skating adrenaline. We laughed about something that happened that evening. As we played out the scenario, Mommy laughed with us interjecting a joke here and there. She asked about the drive home if Tony had given any of our friends a ride home. We responded no. She asked if I had ridden with Phillip since he was coming to the house. I replied yes. She was still smiling and talking as she exited the kitchen commenting that she was glad we had a good time. Moments later she called to me to the living room where she was resting against the wall over by the window. She called me near and motioned as though she needed to whisper something.

When I walked near her, she motioned silence as though we were going to share a secret or whisper about something. Intrigued I tiptoed across the room closer to her. She quietly closed in leaving little space between the two of us. With one hand resting on the wall, she quietly asked me why I rode home in a different vehicle. She asked if Tony gave someone else a ride. When I said no she reminded me that one of our house rules was that we were to come home with the same one we left with unless there were extenuating circumstances, and my wanting to sit next to Phillip and cuddle did not qualify. The house rule kept us connected with each other and the driver. It kept us accountable for each other. If we wanted to go out, we could not ignore the rules set to ensure our safety.

I knew the rule and I thought about it before getting in Phillip's car, I really did, but I figured this would not count and the exception applied since he was my boyfriend and she approved of him. She reminded me that we had to stick with the plan even if it were tough unless it was an emergency or prior approval given. She said with a quiet voice and a sure look as she stepped in even closer in my face, "Do you understand?" I nodded affirmatively; she smiled and stepped back from me. I was holding my breath while she was talking. Then she motioned me to be quiet and pointed instructions to the kitchen where the others were standing. She had been ever so quiet with the chastisement. I took a deep breath and relaxed before coming out of the room. I regained my composure. Mommy was shorter than me, but I respected her authority. It did not seem like a big deal to me, but it was to Mommy, so I made it important regardless to what I thought about it. It seemed pretty major to her. I figured something must have happened to her or a friend of hers when she was younger. The rule came from somewhere and was in place for our safety from something.

I walked outside the room and joined the conversation with others. Mommy walked out of the living room with a smile and headed towards her bedroom. When she was in another room, I told them she had just jacked me up. Denise, Tony, and Phillip stared at me with surprise before busting out in laughter. They could not believe it. They did not hear a thing. They started laughing. Then with a quick pause they thought about it, and they could believe it. We said she was good at what she did. Kudos for her calmness and discretion; no one would have known. Also, I had pulled it together nicely. Why did I tell them? I think I was in shock thinking about what happened. It was embarrassing. I was still dazed at her knockout punch. We kept laughing and acknowledging it was one of the house rules that we always recited aloud before leaving each other so that we got our time and location synchronized. It became our thing, just do it and keep the peace.

TONY TAKES THE MILITARY ROAD

Time seemed to move quickly. It was Tony's senior year of high school, and Denise was already out of the house. She was a freshman in college majoring in psychology at Livingstone College in Salisbury, N.C. Tony and Phillip talked about life after high school. Phillip was determined to go to college and play football, his passion. But where grades had not been an issue for Phillip, Tony had to study, really work at it, but he was confident that it would pay off in the long run. Since his heart's desire from as early as I could remember was to draw professionally, he knew he needed college. He was not sure how to proceed but figured drawing or sketching would be a great career path since he had sketched all of his life and was very good at it. He drew on paper, in the sand, and even in the black dirt outside in the yard. Drawing was his niche. He was sure he could have a career based on his ability to draw and sketch.

The decision to attend college vanished after one conversation with a teacher who discouraged the idea. She assured him that he was not college material. She said his grades had already told the story, and a labor job was more suited for him. Though his grades were average, he assumed there was a school out there that would allow him to draw and design. He was disappointed to find out different. He did not research the matter. He decided she was right.

He told Mommy about the conversation when he arrived home from school disappointed and flustered. Determined to find a new career immediately he asked what he should do. He would not entertain the idea of college from our discussions that weekend although we still suggested it. He said the teacher was not trying to hurt him, and if she felt he did not have what college would need from him, he was not going to waste his time. He began to search for alternatives. It was not the teacher's fault that his grades were not better. He said she sounded matter-of-fact as she pointed out her obvious conclusion. He said he did not want to talk further, and that was that. I could tell his feelings were hurt, but he did not admit it. I did not know if he talked about it to his friends, but our college talk was done. His friends decided on various post-high school ventures including going to college. A few planned to get jobs nearby as they figured out what to do with their lives. Tony tried to figure his next move. The only other desire he had was a career in the military. He mentioned it, but we never even consider it.

His decision came during the Veterans Day season. The movies began to pay homage to the Armed Forces. One movie showed commitment; another movie showed exotic travels; and yet another movie emphasized the strength and character of the men and women in service. There were movies with humor as well as the serious one. Then a military musical movie came on, and I was done. I knew the idea of college had disappeared, and he was hooked. Mommy explained that the military was not his only option, but he insisted it was not an option. He decided this was where he was supposed to be. Tony decided to join the military.

Drawn to images of the army, he committed to it. As the months rolled into springtime, it seemed there were more commercials than ever advertising the kind of personality and drive needed for a soldier to guard what America held dear. Tony liked the idea of being our guardian angel. I envisioned my brother as the soldier in the movies and sometimes I did not like what I saw. It was dangerous. War movies did not intimidate him, but some of them did scare me. I was not as brave or sure of this idea. I wondered what would become of his passion for art. It was safe, and I knew somewhere out in the universe, he was meant to draw. He comforted me explaining if it were meant to be a part of his life, it would show up somewhere. He did not know how or when but he was determined not to worry about it. He asked me to let it go so that there would be no discussions of it while he was out of my sight, and I was alone with Mommy. He was trying to get her to a place of peace with the military idea. He did not need me undermining his choice with my ideas of grandeur for him. He needed the family united behind him. I agreed and apologized citing that my only desire was for his happiness with his choice after the honeymoon wore off and he was stuck in the marriage. He said he was sure of what he was doing and asked me to trust him. That was really all he needed to say because I did trust him. I always relied on him for my direction, and he always supported me. I was not about to let him down when he needed me the most. His words rang in my ears, and I knew what I had to do. Instantly I backed off, dropped the idea of college, and began encouraging the idea of him as a great soldier. He said that was much better.

The idea of the army stimulated a notion of doing something important, and he would get paid training, travel, and a dream. He put art behind him though Mommy was not excited about such a big step. She said if he did not like a course in college he could change it. If he did not like a college, he could always change the school or come home. He would not have that option in the military. Tony said he was not fickle. This was apparently the answer to his prayers, and he was more determined and at peace. But Mommy struggled with the idea.

An even bigger picture formed. Tony wanted to continue helping with the household expenses. Denise was in college, and I was preparing to enter the following year. Mommy tried to assure him it was not his responsibility to provide for the family. He was her son, her child. He insisted he wanted to help the family he loved so much. Mommy spoke of scholarships and grants, but it was a lost battle. By now, Tony liked the idea of being a man, an army man. She could not change his mind, and when she realized this was not a decision of desperation but of honor, she backed off and stood proud with him though her heart ached at the idea.

When Tony graduated high school in June of 1980, he headed to Texas. He entered the military before he graduated high school through an early enlistment program and departed maybe a week after graduation. Mommy cried so much when he left. Denise had entered college a year earlier, but this was different. She came home on school breaks and was only a few hundred miles away. Tony had to leave his family and familiar surroundings. He would go from the nest for sure. That thought probably brought Mommy the greatest pain.

While Tony was away for the first six months, he left his car with me. Denise did not have her driver license, and she was content with that. I was not. I wanted to drive and saw it as a sort of independence. Tony knew how I felt about it, and he gave me the opportunity to have some of that freedom I wanted as a senior in high school. The rest would be up to Mommy. He gave me specific instructions on how to care for his car, and assured me if Mommy told him I was not taking good care of it, he would suspend my use of it. I knew he was serious.

He took very good care of it and left it behind for me during my senior year. It was not an easy decision. I was not offended or annoyed at his instructions. I was on cloud nine. He was serious about my commitment to follow through while he was nowhere around. He said that his rims had to stay cleaned too. He showed me how to clean it, told me which washcloths to use and even the rhythm and motions needed to bring a nice shine and gloss to the paint job. He wanted me to keep it fueled, the oil checked, and serviced it as needed. He wanted to know if I agreed before leaving it in my care. I was glad to do it. This meant I would not have to borrow Mommy's car.

He bought his first car during his sophomore year in high school and worked to pay the car payments and insurance. He drove school bus his sophomore, junior, and senior year of high school and had other jobs during the summer months to pay his expenses. Two years later he traded the first car for a newer model. It was his favorite color—brown and had great features. Now he was leaving it in my care. I was honored that he trusted me with the car. Excitedly I agreed to his terms.

Calling home from El Paso, Texas, Tony spoke with us weekly. He called Mommy about my upcoming high school graduation. I started smiling as I figured out the topic from the discreet comments she made. They wanted it to be a surprise apparently. I slipped out of her sight and walked to her room. Ever so gently picking up the telephone receiver, I listened to their conversation. I knew I should not be eavesdropping, but I wanted to know if my suspicions were correct. I heard them talk of buying a car for me. So excited at the thought, I busted in on their conversation with much thanksgiving. They told me to hang up the phone. Suddenly a strange thought spewed from my mouth. I told them I could not let them do it. I did not want to put a burden on the family just as he had decided against it a year prior. Our heads were above water, and I liked the feel of it. A car sounded nice, but I did not need one. They were shocked, but not as shocked as me.

I told them thanks, but no thanks. I could not afford the upkeep. Unlike him, I did not want to work and pay for a car instead of school or while attending college. I certainly was not asking Mommy to get another job to pay for it or Tony's earnings pay for a car for me. I did not want the worry of insurance, tires, and anything that may occur. It sounded too expensive. I wanted to go to school bottom line. I did not want the sacrifices, and I was honest with them. They asked if I were sure and I said yes. I could not let them take on this expense. I declined the offer of a car.

Like Tony I drove the school bus during my sophomore, junior, and senior years of high school. I helped Mommy with a few small expenses, but I had not purchased a car. The first six months I used Tony's car, and the rest of the year I used Mommy's car when I needed transportation. Denise was in college, and she did not have a car. She managed. For some reason, it was not a big deal. I wondered how he maintained the car, insurance payments, incidentals, and had money for fun. My money was gone shortly after the check cashed, and I bought a few things. I tried to continue with the same good money practices from years prior, but clothes and stuff were so appealing; it was costing me to go window shopping. I was looking and buying.

Denise was better about saving. She loved college, and it seemed to agree with her, but she was not spending every dime she received. She had a great attitude anyway, but she seemed to have even more flare. She spent her money on clothes sometimes, but her dollar bills must have spent different than mine because hers lasted. Neither of us was focused on designer clothes, just nice attractive clothing that we could afford. And she wore it well. I always admired her look. Jo had her own cute look also. She was three years my junior, but she was really into fashions from her early years. Differing from me and Denise, she bought designer things. When our funds lessened near zero, Denise was just a call away. We had to get a small speech sometimes though.

Tony planned to attend my high school graduation. I knew it. There was never an important event when we were not there with each other.

The year prior Tony had graduated from high school, and Denise was home from college to attend. In three more years, JoAnn would graduate and no matter where we were, I knew all would come together for it. We made family important.

A week before graduation Tony came home. I remember the day he drove up in the yard as though it were yesterday. We were all at home that day, Mommy and her three girls. Phillip was attending Livingstone College on a four-year football scholarship. He was home for summer vacation. We were still dating, and he had stopped by. We were outside standing in the yard talking and enjoying the beautiful sunny day while Mommy sat nearby in a lounge chair on the front porch. Phillip remarked that it would be nice if Tony was home with us if he could come home that very day.

In less than five minutes, I saw a car about two blocks from the house and knew it was Tony. As he rounded the curve that would bring him to the driveway, I saw a big smile on his face through the windshield of his Mercury Cougar. We were so excited! It was like the Christmas thrill of a child opening presents. We were jumping up and down while running towards the car as it entered the yard. We waved our hands motioning for him to get out of the car. Grabbing the door handle, he could not get out of the car fast enough for us before Mommy was off the porch and into his arms along with the rest of us still jumping up and down. Phillip stood back and watched the fanfare die down before moving forward to greet him. We were all together again. It was like old times. For that week while Tony was home we had so much fun.

We visited Ma-Ma. She was glad to see all of us but especially Tony. We sat outside on her porch around her knees as she sat in a chair reminiscing about old times and our childhood. We visited her a second time that first week because it felt so good just sitting and talking with Ma-Ma. We could feel her love, and we missed it. It was different seeing her occasionally, whereas she used to be with us every day. That had been some time ago now, and we adjusted to change, but we still missed her. In the past, she was there for us. She was always there. She was so much a part of us. She missed us too. She said we were such clowns because we made her laugh the entire time. When we were together it was as though we had never parted.

On graduation day, our seniors were asked to arrive early in preparation for the ceremony. I did so. Mommy and the gang followed later even though they were dressed before I left the house. After commencement classmates, friends, and I made plans to meet later that evening at a nightclub. As we stood outside in our cap and gowns, one friend said it was the last time all of our classmates would gather together. I disagreed quickly assuring her we could gather for reunions. She said not everyone would attend. Life would take us different places to do different things and we would never all assemble again. She was right. We gave big hugs before saying goodbye.

A lot of us including my brother and sisters were supposed to gather at one location, this youthful spot where the teenagers listened to music, danced, and had fun. We traveled separately but planned to meet sometime that night. We had permission from Mommy. Everyone simply had to know who everyone else was traveling with and our planned time of rendezvous. Phillip was my riding partner as we stopped by his house for a visit with his mom before going to the party. We gathered all week with friends and had so much fun. Graduation night was a continuation of the same.

That night I did not go to the club. After we had talked for a while, Phillip's mom Jean left. We glanced at the TV commenting on the show and decided to watch for a few minutes thinking we had plenty of time to spare. Before long I was sleep. Falling asleep at Phillip's home was an unwelcomed happenstance. I was exhausted but did not realize it. When I woke up I was so disappointed that I missed the gathering. Phillip said he would still take me, but it was late, so I told him to take me home. We arrived first, but Denise and Jo came in shortly afterward. We were all tired, so Phillip left, and we went to bed. Tony was the only one not home yet. We figured one of us had some extra energy and hoped he had a great time.

Awakened by screams from Mommy about two o'clock in the morning, we ran to her bedside frightened. She had a terrible dream about one of us. She would not say what the dream entailed; only that it was horrible. She started frantically asking about each of us. She called each of us by name. Awaiting our response, we answered to the call of our names even though we were standing in front of her by now.

We tried to figure out what was going on. Lastly she called for Tony. We realized he was not standing at the bedside with us. We checked his room. He had not arrived home yet. Mommy started looking around and asking for him. We reminded her he said he was going to be out all night long. It had been a year since he was with his friends. She did not accept that answer. She reminded us that he never disappeared all night and normally did not stay out too late. We told her it was only around two o'clock. We explained we were tired, so we came home early. It was a pretty tiring week. We crammed so much into each day and later found ourselves drained on the night we planned to do the most. Tony was out having fun.

Mommy knew something was wrong. She got out of her bed and headed into the sitting room and began to look around in the house. When she looked up in the sitting room, she saw the clock on the wall. It stopped working only moments ago at the time of her screams. She was sure it was an omen and something was wrong. We tried to calm her and get back to sleep, but we could not. Much time and conversation settled her down enough to get her back in bed for a little while, but she did not sleep.

Away from her, we acknowledged that it seemed wrong to us. I felt sick down in the pit of my stomach. Denise and Jo felt sick too, but we thought part of it could have been from the fright Mommy had just caused. Honestly, I did not know whether she caused it with the shrieks or the stopped clock caused the unrest, but something now seemed terribly wrong. Mommy was right. Tony never stayed out too late. Even though he made that comment, we did not expect it from him.

We had no answers. Later the next morning there was still no sign or Tony. We called some of his friends and asked if they had seen him. When last seen, he was fine. He was a little tired they commented. We kept reminding Mommy that he had said he was going to be out all night. She asked if he called. He had not called. It was not like him, but we figured he had been gone for a year, and this was time to enjoy his friends before returning to Texas. In the morning when we discovered that he was not with friends we became very concerned, scared even. It did not make sense. We could not figure it out. We kept praying for his phone call.

Later that morning Phillip stopped by. He and Tony were supposed to pick up my engagement ring in nearby Elizabeth City. It was a graduation surprise. With plans for the morning and Tony's absence, we knew something must be wrong. He did not just blow off appointments. We tried to stay composed as we told Phillip what happened. Phillip decided to take Mommy, one of her friends, and me with him to pick up the jewelry telling them the purpose of the trip. I was okay with them coming along; after all, I was not supposed to be with him either. It created a temporary diversion, and even though I was so excited about the ring my mind was on my brother. We told Denise and JoAnn to tell Tony to stay put when he arrived. By now the sick feeling in my stomach would not leave. I was scared but tried to act as though I was okay because Mommy was so concerned.

When we returned home that afternoon right after twelve, Tony had not arrived. There was no doubt something was definitely wrong. Mommy kept saying something had happened to her son. We tried to assure her differently needing to convince ourselves too. Mommy, her three girls, and Phillip were once again outside on a beautiful sunny day hoping to see Tony driving his car and rounding the curve as he did just a week ago. About two hours later, a friend of Tony's speedily entered our driveway to give the report. Jumping out of his car leaving the engine running he told us Tony was killed in a car accident. Knocked unconscious in the car he hit the corner of a bridge, overturned into a creek with the car landing upside down, and he drowned in shallow water. He was found still wearing his seat belt less than three miles from home. Tony had fallen asleep at the wheel.

I assured him he was mistaken, but he assured me it was Tony. He was at the scene of the accident with the police and wrecker. I could not believe it. I did not want to believe it. I turned towards Mommy screaming out what he said to me. She ran off the porch and collapsed in Phillip's arms; Denise and JoAnn gathered nearby. We did not want to hear this. Oh my God!

Jo ran in the house and called our neighbors. They came quickly. When we saw them, we were overwhelmed. It started to be real. Denise fainted as they arrived in our yard and I started to scream uncontrollably. I could not close my mouth. A loud long yell rang out from the depths of my soul, and I could not stop. Our neighbor, the mother of the bunch, tried to comfort me, but I was irrational. She shook me several times, but I could not stop screaming. She had slapped me repeatedly before I realized my face was ringing with a numbing pain. I raised my hand slightly to shield my face from the next slap and wept bitterly on her shoulder. They tried to hear the news as Tony's friend tried to tell them what he had just witnessed. Immediately neighbors, friends, and family arrived.

Our dad came when he heard the news and shortly afterwards Aunt Alice and Aunt Maggie did likewise. I overheard them talking at the kitchen table while Mommy was outside on the front porch with other visitors. As they shared their grief, I did not interrupt. Instead, I said a prayer that this would not happen to any other sons of the family, especially my sisters or mine. I prayed for our unborn sons.

Neighbors, friends, and family were affectionately supportive. They rallied quickly from all over the city, state, and east coast as the news reached the communities. The phone rang constantly. Tony's friends Barry and Neil visited and called constantly lending their arms of compassion, as did many of our teenage friends and classmates. Day after day we sat and talked about Tony's life and how dear he was to us. It seemed like a dream, more like a nightmare, but we could not wake up. I did not want this terrible thing to be real, Tony was gone forever. What a cruel thought.

The house was crowded day and night with family and friends until after the funeral. Phillip's family was supportive. Then quiet filled the house. We still received calls and occasional visits, but a silence saturated the rooms that once echoed the many voices. The crowds disappeared. I preferred the noise; that way I did not have to think so much. Laughter was a good trade off from the tears as we joked of happier times. Sadness was imminent.

Mommy sat on the porch quite a bit that summer from early morning to late evening. It seemed to be a place of some comfort to her. She did not work in her flowers. She sat longingly on that porch looking so sad whenever she did not have a task at hand. I asked her about life and death, heaven and hell, and what she thought to be true. I wanted to be mad, but Mommy was not. She was deeply hurt, but she was not angry at God. Tony was only nineteen years old, and his life had ended.

We cried a lot. When I talked tears flowed as though it were a natural occurrence. I did not want to cry around Mommy, Denise or Jo seeing their pain. We tried to cry apart from each other to present a shoulder for each other. He was our brother, best friend, and now he was gone forever. This was not fair. I chased the thoughts. If I had just gone to the club that night, maybe we could have guided each other home through our tiredness, maybe something would be different, and maybe Tony would be alive. These thoughts bombarded my mind.

People kept telling us to be strong. They meant well. I decided to stop crying around them. Phillip took me for drives to be away from everybody for a little while. When Mommy realized what I was doing, she called us together and said to cry whenever we needed. It started our talks again. We sat on the porch a lot with her and just talked. We stayed close to each other. With the grace of God, we made it through. It was tragic and unexpected. It was not fair, but Mommy said life was not always fair. He was a part of us, and we loved him beyond measure. He taught me to count, and I taught him to spell. We helped each other in so many ways. He was always there for me.

I walked slowly passed Tony's bedroom. It was time to give away his things, give them to the needy. In my heart, I wanted to keep everything. I wanted to let his brown leather jacket continue to hang behind the door with the smell of his cologne on it. I wanted to leave his brown hat on the corner of his dresser perfectly creased in the center. I wanted to leave his room the way it had been, but I could not, we could not. So we packed up and gave away his things to be a blessing to someone else.

It felt as though I was giving a part of him away to strangers. They did not know the person who had used those things. They would not know some of those things were his favorites. They would not know the person who loved life and had owned those things. They would never know. But we knew. As we packed each item away, I started feeling selfish again. I wanted to keep his things. Mommy said to keep an item or two was okay, but for the most of it I had to let it go. We talked, cried, laughed, and kept packing until there were no more items to give. When we closed the last box we cried desperately missing him and saying goodbye again. I did not want to, but I had to let those things go. Tony was always with us in our hearts, just a memory away. I love and miss him still.

A CHANGE IN SCENERY

At the end of the summer, one of my friends chose the path of marriage and children rather than college. I was so happy for her and I wished her well, yet I was concerned. I knew family struggle all too well. I did not want her to experience that pain. Her parents were still together. Mommy reminded me. Even though I was engaged to Phillip, I promised myself the education of college. Education would alleviate the pain of being left alone I thought. Mommy assured me that I was speaking through my disappointments. She said education did not guarantee happiness. I should not allow experiences to leave me bitter; instead, learn from them and let them build my character. Assuring me that marriage can work, she said plan for a successful one not its failure. Enjoy life; it was much too short. I knew she was thinking about Tony. "If your girlfriend wants to marry and raise a family, God bless her. She knows what she wants for her life. Support her. She'll do fine. She's a beautiful girl with a good heart, and a nice guy loves her. She will be alright. Pray for her," she said. "Let her follow her own dreams. Everybody doesn't have to think like you, Jackie." I nodded in agreement having heard that before from her. A week later, it was official. My parents were divorced. Five years separated and no attempt to reconcile proved divorce was their agreed solution. They both seemed fine.

It was time for me to go away to college. I was leaving everything behind. Honestly I do not know if I could have made the move if Denise and Phillip were not already attending the college. My heart was home with my family as were many memories of my brother. It was hard to leave home for school. I felt as though I was leaving a part of me. The talks with Mommy, times spent with JoAnn at home were important. I did not want to leave Jo. I kept thinking about Tony. I needed the late night conversations with Mommy and Jo. Now I had to leave them behind. I did not want to do that. This separation was too great. It hurt to think about it. Tony would not ever come home again. His bedroom still reminded me of him even though most of his things were gone. I could not let go of him. Mommy said that I had him with me. He was in my heart and in my memories forever. She said Denise and I needed to go to school.

Denise and I packed our things into trunks and suitcases, and Mommy drove us to college with the U-Haul trailing behind the car. The drive to school was pleasant. Nothing unusual happened. As we arrived my roommate appeared, and we exchanged excitement for the days ahead. I was glad it was one of my classmates from high school. After my things were in the room and Mommy checked school finances, she headed home. Denise stayed with me since she was a part of the welcoming council for the freshman class. She unloaded her things in the upper classman dormitory. I started to breathe a fresh atmosphere of change even though I knew I would miss Mommy and Jo. I did not know how they would make it without Denise or me at the house with them. Phillip was already at school practicing football. I figured eventually I would see him, but for now it was Denise, my roommate Dee, and me.

At school food became a source of comfort. Not able to sleep many nights I sat up, watched television, and ate chips. When my roommate realized what was happening, she stayed up with me and offered conversation as we ate Doritos and Wheat Thins. We talked about Tony. She knew him well since we attended the same high school. She traded her sleep for conversation until I was able to sleep easily. Eventually, we slept after many late nights.

Calling home to check on the family brought comfort. Those were some tough times for Mommy's family, especially for Mommy who now had three children away from home realizing one would not return. The last five years demanded strength with the death of her dad, marriage, oldest sister, mom, cousin, aunt, and now her son. Denise, Jo, and I were very concerned for her.

We popped in for visits home since Phillip drove his car to college. I thought about the car I did not want and how handy it would be at times like these. But Phillip gladly drove the gang home for a quick visit whenever we had a little time off from school and even when it was just for the weekend. Jo would let us know how things were going. We talked with Mommy, but we talked even more with Jo to find out if anything happened that we should know about. We wanted Jo to be okay too. I was glad Mommy insisted I go to school as planned. Finally, we were able to laugh and not feel guilty about being alive.

College life was great. I could go to class at my own discretion. It was my responsibility. And if it were not for the knocks on my door Sunday mornings by the moral compass Denise, Dee and I could have enjoyed lazy Sundays. She reminded me how I was raised in church on Sundays. She was right, and I was eventually glad she did not forget. After church and Sunday brunch the rest of the day belonged to us. I complained, but I looked forward to her coming by the room to aggravate me and keep me grounded in that area.

College life was all around fun. There were so many students from outside the state of North Carolina. Classes were manageable, some even easy, none too difficult, and the camaraderie was priceless. All of that studying demanded by the grown-ups had paid off. Dee fell in love. Phillip was busy with football practically all of the time. I saw him here and there, but his commitment to the game kept him busier than Dee's obligations to band, and Niece's responsibilities with her sorority sisters. Nevertheless, we found time to connect. We valued each other as well as our individual friends. Jo came to visit staying in the dorm an occasional weekend. She was sold on the idea of college at Livingstone. She liked the environment and our friends looked out for her too. Dee and I joined the same sorority as Denise. College life kept us pretty busy.

The summer of '82, Phillip and I planned our wedding; actually, we planned a marriage. Sitting in the living room of my house while everyone else was some other place we talked about commitment to each other. Then he said, "Jackie, we should get married." I said, "Why not? Sounds good to me." The date set was for Valentine's Day of '83.

It sounded romantic but not practical for North Carolina in the winter. The weather could be unpredictable. So we changed the date.

We discussed the specifics of marriage as we understood them. The next few hours we discussed what we wanted in a family, how we felt about infidelity, whether or not we wanted children, how to raise them, where we wanted to live, religion, politics, money, and more. We talked about anything and everything we could think of that would or could pertain to us. Dating two years and engaged for another two years allowed time to learn some things but not everything. We realized there was more to discuss, so we tried to find those topics and talk about them. We discussed what we wanted out of life and what we were willing to do to get it. We talked about what we would not tolerate. That was interesting. We talked about church although, at the time, neither of us was very committed to attending. There was a future plan which involved the church. We believed in God. There was no doubt about that. This topic warranted additional conversation. We discussed attending the same church as opposed to the way we grew up with one parent in one church and the other in another. We talked about sex. We discussed each topic until we agreed. It was not overwhelming, it seemed natural. We laid the ground rules. At the end of the conversation, we were satisfied with our answers.

In a few days, we would return to school from winter break. I was nineteen and Phillip twenty; however, in a week I would be twenty and the end of February Phillip would be twenty-one. We wanted to support each other's goals. We figured out how to disagree without falling apart. There would be no violence, none. We laughed as we discussed some pretty heavy subjects, but we were serious. By the end of the afternoon, we were ready to announce our decision to marry.

Walking out of one room finding family in the other room and outside, we shared the good news with them. They were thrilled; however, we realized we needed time to plan the wedding we wanted. There were relatives up north that we wanted to be a part of the celebration and winter could prevent it. Therefore, we changed the date to July 30, 1983.

Phillip's mom was excited at the news too. A summer wedding sounded great. The moms offered help in any capacity agreeing that a winter wedding, though beautiful, meant some friends and relatives in other places may not be able to attend. We decided it was more important to have loved ones with us rather than a picturesque winter wedding.

Mommy said she had to have a talk with me. She started with how much she loved Phillip and the idea of us getting married. She continued. Each marriage was different. I had to be honest with myself and with my husband. Love him unselfishly not demanding my way all of the time. She said not to compare him with anyone else; my relationship should be sacred. It required sacrifice. It would not work without forgiveness. She knew I loved Phillip, but it was more than a feeling. She said keep folk out of my business. Do not sit around and complain about your husband. People are not so forgiving even when you forgive and move on. Pray about it instead of so much talk about it. Then she was done. The conversation was over. I had little input, and that is how she wanted it. She just wanted me to listen with seriousness.

There was so much to do with the wedding date seven months away and Mommy and I with our own tasks in different locations. I was back in school in Salisbury, and Mommy was six hours away at home in Sunbury. She found a dress I may like, but I had to come home to see it. We selected invitations already; Phillip said he liked them, so they were ordered. He did not have much interest in the logistics of the wedding. He said whatever I wanted he wanted me to have, and I was not offended. I shared information and asked his opinion, and if he wanted to give input, that was fine and if he had none, that was fine too. We kept the momentum flowing. Mommy and I were focused. She told me not to worry about the cost of the wedding, but she knew I would not be extravagant on her dime. I was mindful. She had no complaints and together we made it work. When I came home to look at the gown, it was gone. I waited too long, but I was not worried. I knew I would find the perfect gown, and I did. It was purchased, fitted, and stored for a later date. There was no wedding drama. Things went along smoothly.

Four months later the wedding day arrived. Everyone was in place at the church, and we started on time though my wedding planner suggested a delayed entrance for the bride. I declined because it seemed unfair to have someone wait for me at the altar while I delayed on purpose. The music played as I searched from my position at the back of the church for Phillip at the front. I looked pass the well-wishers in the pews. I could not see him, but I knew he was there.

Though my dad was there, I wanted to walk down the aisle unescorted. Helen, one of my best friends from high school, flew in to stand as maid of honor. Denise, JoAnn, and Phillip's sister Stephanie were bridesmaids. Phillip's brothers, Michael and Stephen, were groomsmen. His siblings were six and seven years younger than him, but still groomsmen and bridesmaid. Stephen and Stephanie were the twins in the bunch. Other family and friends occupied the other spaces of bridesmaids and groomsmen. Phillip's dad Mike was best man. Moms of the bride and groom, Grandmothers Ma-Ma, Grandma Hattie, and Grandma Inez were seated for the ceremony.

I proceeded down the aisle as directed after taking a deep breath. Dressed in a long white wedding gown, I walked and prayed to God that this would be the perfect day for us. This was my last quiet intimate moment before becoming a Mrs., and I needed focus and clarity. Even though I smiled with every step, a prayer was said, a big one. Being a clumsy child, one would think it foolish, but it was my desire. Though my gown was long, it was not underfoot as I walked. I believed Phillip was the one for me, but I prayed that should it be wrong, my answer would come before I reached him at the front of the church. I prayed this was the right thing and the right time for us. While smiling at the guests, I continued to pray. My request to God was as drastic as it needed to be. This time, I did not mind the embarrassment. I prayed; I wanted a sign before I reached Phillip at the altar. I prayed to trip, fall, and any kind of sign if we missed the mark. Let it end before it began. I prayed believing I would have my answer and prepared to back out of it if I needed to do so. This was a private conversation; I wanted no one else's opinion about my prayer.

Arriving at the front of the church intact seeing Phillip's smile and reassurance in his eyes I knew I had my answer from God. I knew it was the right decision come what may. This day, this moment, and the two of us were in the right place. Destiny looked good. It was time to live our dreams. Phillip proved to be a guy of good character and gentle towards me. I wanted to be his wife and mother of his children in the distant future. I wanted to travel with him different places and so more but the first thing was first. We needed to complete the ceremony. Reverend Moore proceeded, we vowed, and it was done.

We said our *I do's* before God and the crowd. We kissed, exited the church, jumped in his yellow Mercury Capri, and drove to the reception hall 40 miles away. We said we did not feel different as we honked our horn repeatedly and waved our arms out of our windows drawing attention to our just married signs on the car. We said it was because we were married in our hearts before the formality. This made it official, and let everyone else know.

We knew we made mistakes in our pasts and more were sure to come, but we decided to let go of the past and not worry about the future. Today we would celebrate love. We kissed again, blew the horn, and drove off disappearing so fast that we missed our photo shots with the wedding party. They were still waiting for us to re-enter the church. When they realized we left, they said they figured we would come back and take pictures. Everyone was looking for the bride and groom. We gave it no thought until we arrived at the reception hall and realized no one had followed. Here was our first mistake. There was no easy way to rectify this. We just messed up. We burst into laughter because the reception hall was an hour drive from the church. We could not go back because they would be coming to the reception hall. The pictures were a loss we had to accept. We hoped they took pictures without us. Another option was to take photos at the reception hall.

Phillip and I were blessed with the good fortune of not having in-law drama. Mommy and Jean (Eugenia's nickname) became good friends. Both of them loved both of us and were more than fair. No one could hope for more. We often told friends about our treasured in-laws. We lived between the two families for the rest of that summer. Phillip did not return to college after his junior year. He worked with his dad in the family logging business while deciding on the next venture.

Denise graduated in May but did not have a job yet. She was deciding what to do when she remembered a military recruiter stopped by the school for career day. He told her of the advantages of joining the armed forces using her college degree; with no offers in hand she gave the recruiters' invitation serious thought. She talked with a recruiter several times. Mommy reminded her that she liked to dress nice for every trip outside her front or back door even for a trip to the corner store. I reminded her that she did not even go to the mailbox without being flawlessly put together. Jo said that she just could not see it happening. In the military Denise would run, sweat, get dirty, and not have a chance to get it together until the mission was completed. This would happen in basic training before even getting to the career. Had she forgotten that she was very attentive about gracefulness? Denise said she was prepared and could make the adjustment. I did not believe it since she had been meticulous since she was about six years old or even earlier. She had always been that way. Every scenario we offered she countered with necessity. We were surprised but finally embraced the idea of Denise joining the military. It had a strange ring, but we were supportive none the less.

She asked us to accompany her to visit the recruiter. Phillip stopped by that Saturday afternoon, so we took him along also. He agreed to go interested to see how this turned out. The five of us loaded up in Mommy's car and visited the recruiter's office in Elizabeth City. While talking with the recruiter for about twenty minutes Denise decided against it, but the recruiter was not distracted. He focused on Phillip now that Denise was certain this was not what she wanted to do. Without missing a beat, he continued flow of conversation assuring her that her decision was not a character flaw but just not where she needed to be right now. He turned to Phillip rotating in his chair slightly still having the view of all of us as he spoke of the importance of being in the right place at the right time and being fulfilled. He discussed the pros and cons of the military and the benefits of military family life. Since Phillip and I both wanted to travel, we agreed it was the career path for Phillip instead of Denise. I could travel with him whenever assigned a family tour of duty. We listened as the recruiter discussed the possibilities.

Sacrifice was a part of military family life, and he wanted to make sure he was not giving us the impression that Phillip would have a regular job like the civilian sector. He said he wanted to be realistic as he smiled, joked, and still somehow seriously explained the charge. We were at ease as he discussed our lives. We had to willingly part from each other as the mission dictated.

I liked this sergeant because he did not pacify me but spoke of what Phillip needed from me and said he was glad I was there with him so he could give me an accurate depiction of military family life as well as let me know what my husband would experience. Phillip would not just learn the military weapons; he may have to use them in wartime. Phillip could further his education and travel. We would have plenty of fun time but had to be willing to pay the price.

I remembered my conversations with Tony about some of the same issues minus the wife part. It had been Tony's choice, and now it was Phillip's choice. This felt right for us but only if Phillip said it was right for him. Suddenly our lives got bigger. It was a little overwhelming as we discussed that we only went to the recruiter's office for Denise. We had no idea how the day would unfold. Our dreams and ground rules paved the way with Denise's help. Excitedly Phillip thanked Denise for asking him to come along. We joked with her that she knew she was bringing a tradeoff so she could tell the recruiter in person that she changed her mind. A week later I returned to college a married woman, a junior, and the wife of a military man. What a summer. Phillip continued work with his dad while he awaited the departure date for basic training.

Our families did not want us to move away but did not try to stop us. With two years of college left, my plan was to finish school. Phillip had basic and other training before we could think about living together. We would pass in the night for a while, but the school eventually ended for both of us. We said we were still happy with our recent decisions. We just had to stay focus.

Mommy and Jean were kindred spirits. Though they had never spent time together as friends prior to their children's relationship, they realized they knew many of the same people. They became family to each other leaving us behind as they visited relatives. They were comfortable making new acquaintances. Both of them had a powerful love for their own families. Jean was with her family most of the time just like Mommy. Occasionally the moms shopped together. They visited each other's church and religious functions. Like I said, it was a blessing.

Our families grew closer until Phillip and I were unable to imagine it any other way. Some people did not understand it and questioned loyalties assuring me the in-laws would turn on the both of us. Some said it could not be genuine, it had to be pretense, but we did not allow their opinions to cloud our judgment. We knew they were speaking advice from a place in their hearts and minds where they had been wounded or witnessed it with other family members or friends. It did not have to be that way. We refused to endorse the stereotypes. When we heard the in-law jokes, we discouraged them and shared our stories sometimes. We understood they meant no harm; they were just sharing their experiences and some had ugly stories. They did not believe it was possible to have great relationships with in-laws. Many did not have healthy marriages because of in-law hassles. But that was not our story. Our mothers were committed to supporting us. We appreciated them and tried not to complain too much to them. They were not trying to hear it anyway.

DON'T WHINE ABOUT IT

Phillip and I made the commitment, but there were things we did not know about each other. We dated four years before marriage and thought that told us a lot about each other, but Mommy was right. There was still more to learn, and though we felt we knew enough, twenty and twenty-one was definitely not old. We were young with a lot to discover about living together. Not every question surfaced that day in my living room. Our moms had already refused our whining. Mommy would not allow fussing about Phillip and the toothpaste or leaving the toilet seat up. The socks outside the hamper were not worthy of a good argument. She said that was minor stuff. "Pick your battles and that's not one," she said. If I were going to tell the story, I had to tell the whole story. She said there were three sides to every story; mine, his, and the truth. The truth usually got a bum rap because we did not tell everything that happened. She said many times we may not even think about the entire story, only our point of view. Phillip folding towels his way instead of mine after I told him how I wanted them did not constitute war. She said to work it out and think about what to say before trying to go out in a blaze of glory. I did not want to hear all of that. She denied my ego. And she did not want to hear me whine about my growing pains. She refused to see me without fault which angered me sometimes. She said, "I know you, Jackie. Don't play innocent."

With our moms standing in their own corners refusing to pick a winner, we decided to work through stuff. We talked about not getting others involved in our disputes. It would not be fair to our siblings. Denise was finding her career. JoAnn was a seventeen year old high school senior. Michael (Butch) and Steve and Stephanie (the twins) were younger than Jo, so they did not care about this stuff. There was no need to drag the siblings in our disputes or our high school and college friends. So we decided to fix our own messes. I talked about the relationship with others, but we trusted each other to figure it out. And I relied on a little prayer. Mommy and Jean said marriage was cooperation. I had to compromise. I was not a fan of that although I loved a good bargain. Real life had problems. It was supposed to be that way. Phillip and I were apart two weeks at a time visiting each other on weekends. When he left for the military, we talked occasionally and saw each other even less. It was really challenging, but I kept remembering my promises to Phillip. He seemed to be handling it better than me. We agreed to be sensible, but I was irrational.

I wondered why I was arguing. There was a better way. We always had fun together. We had fun when we were not arguing whether we had money or not. We had a great sense of humor. We did not need money to be entertained. Something was wrong. I was in North Carolina, and he was in Alabama. It was not the ideal situation, but we agreed to deal with it. We started telling silly jokes to break the tension. I began to pray more than a minute here and there turning to the faith that had comforted me in times past. I needed a remedy to alleviate the frustration. I did not want to hurt my friend as I learned things about myself. I needed a way to handle the separation before the rest of our lives kicked in. The confidence I felt about our decisions needed to surface again. I had to live in the moment knowing the good would outweigh the bad.

I decided to minimize the arguments. That alone was a very big deal. There were other ways of showing I missed my husband, and I had to get back on track. We were too far apart to fall apart knowing that we loved each other. Besides we were just getting started. The honeymoon was great, but this part was pressing on the wrong nerve. I thought about Mommy's advice. I did not understand why I liked to fuss in the first place. I always hated it when I saw it at home. Angry at the new me, I changed my attitude instead of blowing up and sounding off. Just a few seconds of word-placement made a world of difference. After overcoming this obstacle, I talked to Mommy and Jean about it. They were glad that I was happy, and things were working out.

The next summer JoAnn graduated high school. Denise and I were home for the ceremony. Denise was living in Maryland but made sure she was available for Jo's graduation. Mommy was thankful her last child was graduating high school. When we were younger college was preached, but Mommy decided to let Jo make her own decision while nudging forward. Phillip could not return for the graduation. He was stationed at Ft. Riley, Kansas and his leave was approved for a few months later. Jo understood. She was glad to see us, but she missed Tony.

At the end of junior year I completed a summer internship in Washington, D.C. Shortly afterwards, I decided to join Phillip in Kansas. By the time I was packed, I decided to make the move permanent. I needed less than ten hours to qualify for graduation, but my thoughts were on spending time with Phillip. Mommy and Jean did not say a thing to us about the decision. Phillip came to get me and with a packed U-Haul we drove to Ogden, Kansas. It seemed the right choice for us at the time as I discussed enjoying and exploring married life.

The military community was very friendly and welcomed me. I met Phillip's friends and their wives. They usually gathered weekly for barbecues and cookouts when the guys were not away on a maneuver. When I arrived, we just continued with the same flow. While Phillip was away I visited my new girlfriends. They were from Kansas, Arkansas, California, Texas, Illinois, and North Carolina. We shopped, ate, and socialized together almost daily. Most of our large circle of friends were moms. Our army husbands brought us together, and friendships kept us busy while the guys were on assignments. At Fort Riley, there was always some soldiering going on.

The environment was much different from college life. It was fun getting to know everyone and hear their stories, but I felt overwhelmed. These ladies were wives and mothers with tiny tots underfoot. They were well-educated in the mission of service. I was not used to this lifestyle or its demands. Phillip and I had been married for a year, but we lived apart while he did basic training and AIT before getting his permanent assignment at Ft. Riley. I was on campus. We saw each other every two weeks then on occasions, but this was our first time actually living together in our own space.

The ladies had children. The children requested attention. I was outmatched as they patted my legs to request water, candy, bathroom, and answers to their questions of why. Their moms looked on laughing as I tried to find my footing, keep my patience, and respond to the toddlers. I was not used to babies. It was hilarious. I had not been around them for any long period of time. Babysitting older children was not the same as meeting the needs of toddlers.

A couple of months later while Phillip and I ate Thanksgiving dinner we talked about college. It was my decision to leave, but now I wanted to return. As we talked, I hoped for the best outcome. I had to find out. Phillip was optimistic. I called the school to make sure I could return to complete my last semester. I was assured I could return. There was a problem; the dorms were already full. I had to find alternative housing. One of the staff personnel suggested contacting different boarding houses and apartments to find vacancies. She offered the name of an elderly lady, a retired educator in the community who offered a room to college students. It was a large bedroom with a full bath situated apart from the rest of the house. She may have an opening.

I started getting excited. I prayed there was space. The lady sounded so nice that I was glad to agree to her terms and stay with her for the final semester. The room was available. Everything was moving fast. I called Mommy with the news and asked if I could come home before going back to school. She was ecstatic. She said she was glad I would finish college but did not want to interfere. We needed some time together. The semester away from school was a sound investment, but it was time to finish what I started at Livingstone. Phillip and I agreed.

I flew home for a few days before leaving for college. When I arrived, JoAnn and her husband Terrence greeted me with their beautiful baby boy Terrence Jr. or TJ. He was two months old. He was the first baby added to our family since the birth of his mom. Those angelic cries sounded musical when I first arrived home. I missed the children from Kansas, but by bedtime I was looking frantically for a pacifier for my precious little nephew's mouth. Thank God for the pacifier. It became one of my best short-term friends. Mommy, Jo, TJ, and I traveled five and a half hours to college to check out the off campus living arrangement. My stay was with the sweet elderly lady named Mrs. Taggart who lived near the campus. Mommy and Mrs. Taggart bonded instantly; they had talked for hours before Mommy and crew returned home. She thanked her for opening her home for the next five months and assured her I would be the perfect house guest. It felt a little like school back in the day when my mom made the visits on the first day of school. I was very comfortable with their meeting. I was thrilled to be at Mrs. Taggart's because it seemed like home. It was a relaxed environment as she shared the stories of her life.

Phillip was unable to travel with me on this trip. I felt a little awkward going to class. I was not sure where I fit in as I returned from military family life. It was clearly my issue. I was living within walking distance from campus instead of sharing a dorm room. Friends welcomed me back to school and caught me up on things I missed. The 'welcome back' reception made life easier. I was glad. Finally, it felt good to be back in the groove of college life. I missed Phillip, but it was comfortable around friends and school again. Salisbury had been home for three years as my friends and I studied and lived together. I was glad to be back.

Five months later Phillip arrived for my graduation. He arrived a few days before the rest of the families including Cousin Buckey who lived in New York. He was one of my mom's beloved first cousins who came home for this graduation just like he did for my high school graduation and wedding. He was like an uncle. Daddy made the trip. I was surprised to see him since he and I had no communication for some time. My parents stayed in touch keeping track of us. My entire immediate family and Phillip's family were there except the grandmas. We thanked everyone for being there for the special occasion each had a hand in bringing to fruition. It was worth returning to school. I was thankful. After graduation, we departed to northeastern North Carolina. Denise only had a few days before returning to work as a health care professional. Phillip and I stayed a little longer before returning to Kansas.

Jo and her baby boy headed home to her husband. It sounded odd as I held the newest member of our family in my arms. Jo was our baby, and she was now wife and a mom. Her son was full of energy and almost a year old. The young parents were watchful ensuring we were not too rough as we played with their son. They were right to check me out since I knew nothing about babies. A baby for us was more than we could imagine at that moment. With another diploma in hand and ready for the workforce, I played with our nephew and planned a long wait before parenting time. At eighteen, Jo married a few months after her graduation practically surprising everyone. They lived with Mommy, and she helped Jo with child-rearing. We were now grown-ups like the people we talked about as children. Us as adults… tree climbing, rope jumping, trick playing, mischievous little people had stepped into the life of adulthood. Wow.

After every phone call to Niece, Tony, Jo, or me, Mommy signed off with, "Don't forget to pray." It continued from childhood when we stayed with our grandparents or our Aunt Mary. It continued through college, army life, living in Maryland, and Kansas. It was needful. She was so intuitive concerning our lives.

One night my mom called me from North Carolina to inform me that I was pregnant. I said, "Mommy, I don't think so." I graduated college a few months ago and used birth control since we were not planning to add to our family for another four years. We wanted to be settled and saved money before having children. At my last check-up, the doctor said conception may be difficult due to prolonged use of birth control. When Mommy said the word pregnant, I assured her it was not me. She should talk to Jo or Denise. She said okay and stopped pressing the issue.

My friends in Kansas thought my mom was correct when I told them about our conversation. They joked that it was my turn, but I assured them emphatically that my body could not do that. They paused and then continued to laugh. They said plans change all of the time.

A week later I started feeling tired. I believed it was because of the stress of looking for a job in the Midwest and not finding one. I had job offers on the east coast before graduation but not in Kansas. The rejection was unsettling. My desire changed from wanting a career to wanting a job. I figured this stress was affecting my energy. Five of the seven wives in our seven couple circle were pregnant at the time. One couple after another got the news, and I was not amused at the domino effect. Even though all but one of them had an older child and knew the symptoms, I rejected the notion. It was not the plan.

About two weeks later I felt worse with body aches. I was sure it was a viral infection due to the environmental change. Maybe depression was the problem. A few days later Phillip left on a field maneuver for two weeks, and my stress level increased. Finally listening to the suggestion of the young wives, I visited one of the military doctors. His quick results confirmed that I was pregnant. He answered me before he received the results of the test assuring that the results would confirm his observation. A call from him with the results came right after I arrived home.

I sat down slowly on the couch trying to digest his comments. My mind started racing. This was not the plan. It was not the time for a baby. We did not have things in place. We were not able to give everything a child needed. As a recent college graduate, my career had not started, and it seemed to be over. A baby meant change. I looked around the room and saw nothing that resembled motherhood. What about our plans? Would I even be a good mother? My mind was racing too fast. Taking a deep breath I closed my eyes and said aloud, "Stop thinking, just stop."

The phone rang at that moment. It was Phillip. He had a break in his schedule, and I had been on his mind. Reluctantly I shared the news from the doctor. Phillip was excited. He tried to convince me to go to the doctor before he left. He shouted the report back to his friends and colleagues and received many congratulatory shouts. He said it was good news. It was okay, and the finances were okay too. He asked, "What about you Jackie? Are you okay? Did the doctor say you and the baby are okay? You've got to take care of yourself, and I'll see you soon." I assured him I was fine smiling big. After talking a while longer, we hung up.

I called my mom to tell her the news. She was so excited. Even though she knew I wanted a career right away, she said the family had to be my first priority. A child was depending on me. It took a few minutes to absorb the idea of a baby. Seldom did things happen exactly as planned. Keep living; there is more to come, she said. She did not say I told you so.

Phillip and Mommy knew me best, and I had talked to both of them that evening. There was never a doubt that we wanted children one day in the distant future; timing was the issue. We wanted to be older and wiser with financial stability and lots of living under our belt. Taking deep breaths I tried to figure our next move. The television noise was unheard in the background. I grabbed a pen and pad off the table in front of me and started writing down our bills. Other thoughts rushed in. I wondered whom the child would look like. I hoped for a girl, and I knew Phillip wanted a boy. Stretching out on the couch I began to think about our lives with a baby, a girl that looked like me or a boy that looked like his dad. Laying the pad and pen aside I smiled placing both hands on my stomach. I thought about a little Phillip or Jackie. Could we do this? We could do this. I could be a mother, be a good mother. I had great examples in my family. I snickered about my thoughts, glad that there was no one with me to witness my craziness. It was not the Kansas temperature or the job stress or even my cooking. It was a baby. What would I say to my friends?

We called Jean with the news when Phillip returned from his field exercise. He wanted to be present for the phone call to his mom with the news. Delighted she asked if we needed anything. We assured her we were okay. Mommy shared the news with Jo and I called Denise. Everybody was happy. Jean and Mommy asked if we wanted them to come to Kansas before the baby was due because of Phillip's frequent field maneuvers. They did not want me to be alone. I declined their offer grateful for the offer knowing their fear of flying. "Y'all, I'm just having a baby. Most of the wives I constantly talked with already had a baby. If I need something, I'm sure they will be here for me. But thanks for the offer," I said with confidence. Childbirth was quite frequent at Fort Riley.

When I shared the news with the ladies I was ready for teasing and laughter, and it happened. They reminded me of things I said about having a baby: it was not going to happen to me, I was waiting for at least four years, and how stress affected the body. Family life changed some of their plans, but they were still planning. They simply fine-tuned as needed. This ladies' talk reminded me of some of the things Mommy said in our previous conversations.

I was not the only person enduring change. They were away from their families too. They were working, having children, and changing careers based on the assignment of their husbands. They were making great sacrifices, and they were not really complaining about it. I decided to be a better friend by listening and observing more. The new attitude created friends for life.

Phillip asked me to wait until after the baby was born before starting a job. I knew this meant postpone work for a year. We had six months before the baby was due and I needed six months after before being comfortable with a sitter. My career would have to wait. I deliberated on that idea for a while. This would be one of many sacrifices I would have to make as a mother. After talking to Mommy, I decided I could live with this decision. I started understanding the young mothers even more and the sacrifices they were undergoing daily while supporting their military husbands. There was a high price to pay for military family life.

I decided to get secure and comfortable in my neighborhood, know the surroundings. I explored the city of Ogden and the Fort Riley installation. I was tired of waiting for opportunity, tired of hoping for a great job offer. The job did not come, and now it would have to wait. Since Kansas was a home away from home, it was time to check out the scenes and shopping stores. The land was flat but pretty. It was different from the east coast, but I liked it. I had never thought of living in the west before Phillip's tour, but I was settling in. I would make it an attractive haven for my family. Phillip and I drove through the countryside having picnics and site-seeing when time allowed him. I loved to drive so when he was away, and the car was with me, driving was a favorite pastime. I refused to be confined to the house. Between friends and explorations, time was moving along nicely. The next two and a half months passed uneventful, pregnant and doing fine. But the following month Phillip's company was assigned a training exercise that would take them to Germany. That scared me. I put on a great face before the moms about having a baby as though it was relatively easy, but it was getting uncomfortable. One day soon, the baby would be born to a mom who had only read about what to do instead of practicing on my friends' children. I started crying, and I did not like it—the crying I mean. I was not emotional like that. There was nothing sad happening at the moment. Why were there tears falling from my eyes? I was becoming more sensitive. I felt as though I was losing control of the situation. I read about it, but figured it would not happen to me. The longer the baby stayed inside, the better we both were. I knew nothing about babies and diapers and what they needed or how to comfort them. Some stuff looked pretty easy, but that crying was a separate matter. The scariest part was to be alone if Phillip did not return before I delivered. I did not want him to worry about me, but I was worried about him being so far away. His commander assured us expectant wives that our husbands would be home before our scheduled deliveries. There was a large population of expectant mothers during this time at Fort Riley.

I was around six months pregnant when Phillip had to leave. With the ninth month approaching, our moms were continuously calling to check on his return date. They did not want me alone, and they definitely wanted him back safely. Assuring them that the situation was under control and Phillip was okay, I checked out more books from the library about childbirth and the newborn. Weeks before the due date Phillip was still overseas, but his commander was trying to get him home. A week later Phillip was still not home though most of the other expectant fathers had arrived. His particular area of expertise required he remain a while longer. I was glad for moms with their spouses but still wondered if Phillip would be as fortunate as the other fathers. With his particular kind of work and the military efforts to return home, I realized it sounded selfish focusing on me all of the time. The snowstorms delayed flights in Europe. Phillip was caught in the weather perils. The baby was coming, and that required my attention.

Jo was pregnant with her second child and scheduled to deliver in a couple of months. We did not talk about our pregnancies, not at first. There were no questions about what to expect although she had been through it. I did not ask Mommy or Jean. I tried to act as though life was unaffected when I talked to them, as though nothing had changed. It was quite obvious that the dynamics of life were full of change. I wanted to prove I could handle it easily.

I saw the military wives practically daily. They volunteered information of their previous pregnancies and deliveries. I wanted to know but did not want to know. I was being pigheaded. The army wives helped anyway providing unrequested information. We were all about the same age. I was twenty-two and sure I could get through this moment if I kept reading and watching these ladies. Sometimes I felt this way, other times I felt completely helpless.

I learned a lot while Phillip was away. Jo and I started talking about motherhood while Jean and Mommy began mailing boxes of unisex infant outfits. Jo had so much she could teach me about birthing and parenting. She was the little sister but not in regard to motherhood. Our talks were good for the both of us. The army wives were my family too, and they would not let me go through even the hormonal woes without giving tips. All of the ladies were determined to prepare me for the journey with laughter and whatever else they could think to give. Finally, I was glad to receive it all. Tell me more, I insisted from everybody just wanting to be prepared. There was no time to be stubborn now, time was short, and the evidence of change was getting heavier each day as the baby began to assume the position. I was not scared, but those stories of pain were an eye-opener as the ladies learned to laugh about it even as they had just given birth.

Our mother's circle was full of practically everything I needed. The young moms delivered the babies about two to three months apart. Two of the moms previously had one girl each before I met them, but those that were pregnant at this time, all six, had boys and one mother had twin boys. Now it was my turn. My philosophy had changed, and I was willing to help out with the children. It was not their fault that my career had not started the way I planned. It was so unfair to punish my friends for my frustrations. Besides, their babies were beautiful.

Phillip arrived home safely on a Sunday, and the baby was waiting for him. He timed it perfect. He was just starting to relax seated on the couch with his eyes closed and head laid back on Monday evening when the labor pains began. I was in the kitchen preparing dinner when I dropped the large spoon that stirred the macaroni and cheese. I grabbed the back of a nearby chair as the pain hammered through my body. I thought the pain would be in the belly region, but I could feel this pain in my toes. As I grabbed my stomach and called for Phillip, I knew this pain was the intense agony I expected. He heard, "I think I'm in labor and this stuff hurts." Phillip said with assurance that I could take the pain but then turned and saw my face. Moments later the pain subsided. He settled back on the couch as I calmed down. Fifteen minutes later, another pain joined us. Phillip asked if he could help. I articulated perfectly how he had already helped. He asked about following the instructions I read in the books. Anger flashed though I was the one who had previously declared it was not a big deal. A book was the last thing on my mind.

Later that night we went to the hospital, but the doctor sent us back saying it was not time. I thought he was zonkers. The pains became less frequent showing up every twenty-four minutes to half hour. The intensity diminished. It was false labor like the doctor diagnosed, and I was just frustrated. Our moms insisted walks would summon the baby's arrival. The pains continued through Tuesday as I walked up and down stairways, took long walks, and every other remedy suggested by anybody. We checked to make sure we had everything in place for the baby's arrival. I was so grateful Phillip was home. I started dinner, but labor pains sent us back to the hospital. Slow dilation, but the labor intensified as the water broke. Something was wrong. I watched every contraction on the monitor screen. I prayed for fast dilation and a quick delivery like most of the ladies experienced, but it was not working that way for me. The baby's heart rate was dropping, and he was in danger. The doctor explained the next step.

Wednesday morning a beautiful healthy baby boy weighing eight pounds, eight and a half ounces was born by caesarean birth. Phillip Jr was born the day after Mommy's birthday. Our baby was finally here, and we were thrilled. Phillip snapped pictures with the camera, and I looked a mess. Hair out of place, exhausted, at my worse, all unnoticed as he photographed the moment. He said I looked beautiful. I knew he was thrilled by the circumstances and not seeing with his natural eyes or he would have set the camera down, and said, "Baby, I'm getting ready to take the picture you will see for a lifetime. Get yourself presentable." Instead, the camera kept flickering in my face.

Phil Jr stared at me that day whenever he was in my arms. He was awake a lot! The next day his eyes followed me around the room. He was so alert that I wondered if it were standard. The doctor and nurse assured me that he saw only the light and the darkness; he could be following my voice. I smiled and did not dispute what they said knowing this baby was different from the rest. He looked directly at me as though he knew me. I tested him repeatedly when they left the room. I decided not to argue with the professionals. It would be our secret. I smiled and kissed his cheeks cradling him as close to me as possible without hurting him. This was my baby, and I was overwhelmed.

In the spring, Jo delivered her second beautiful baby, a son, Antonio, named after Tony. He was healthy too. It was nice contemplating being home with my son playing with Jo's two sons. She handled it like a champ. Mommy was with her for this birth too. I was glad. Now Mommy had three grandsons to keep her busy. A few months later Mommy visited Denise in Maryland and decided to relocate to Washington, D.C. She moved near friends and only a few miles away from Denise. She said she was giving Jo the space she needed to raise her family, and she was ready for a change. Jo stayed at home with her family. This was a significant Mommy move leaving the country-life behind, but she stayed in touch with family and friends ready for a new challenge in her own life.

Thirteen months later I was pregnant again. With this pregnancy, I knew before Mommy called. I think I had known before she did, but I cannot be sure. Because the baby was growing considerably, by six months the doctor tested to make sure all was well and to ascertain if there were multiple babies. Everything was fine. A big healthy baby boy was expected.

This time I was not at the library searching for How to books; I respected what Mommy, Jean, Jo, and the young wives club had to share. It seemed backwards but for whatever reason I was willing to listen to what others had to say about having a baby and childrearing. I was still growing up. They knew a lot about children and their remedies worked. I definitely needed advice on time management.

STILL CONNECTED

One friend suggested the name Stephen Michael after Phillip's brothers Stephen and Michael. The combination names were perfect. Also, it paid homage to Phillip's dad and granddad who shared the name Mike. Stephen and Stephanie visited us in Kansas for their summer breaks. Denise visited as well taking at least a week vacation with us during the summers while we lived there four years. Our parents did not visit, and that was okay. They did not like the idea of a Midwest flight or a ride in a car or bus for that distance. It felt good to have family from home with us. We did not visit home often.

Phillip received orders to leave Fort Riley in my ninth month. The permanent change of duty station was for Fort McPherson in Atlanta, Georgia. At one of the final checkups, the doctor suggested a delayed move, but we insisted the winter January trip would not be too stressful for our newborn or me. Unfortunately, the doctor had a family emergency and said another doctor would deliver the baby. I did not welcome that change but understood it could not be helped.

The weather report forecasted snow. Meanwhile, the movers packed our household goods. We moved into the guest housing at Fort Riley with plans to leave Kansas and drive to Georgia two weeks after the birth. I wondered if we made the right decision. I was determined to be up for the drive. It sounded manageable until the snowstorm came with such vigor.

The contractions began not long after moving into the guest quarters. I lay on the bed while Phillip played a Nintendo game. Phil Jr., now twenty-three months old, sat on the floor beside his dad holding a control supposing that he was also in the game. His dad urged him in game-playing though his control was not actually plugged in. I was tired although not from exerting too much energy. The first time around created a sense of expertise for Phillip. He asked if the labor pains were real or false labor as experienced with Phil Jr. Facing me, he offered jokes for comfort at my expense. It worked as we laughed and talked about Phil Jr. playing the game. He said, with leftover enthusiasm from his game, "When the pains are closer, let me know." The hospital was walking distance under normal circumstances, but with the snowstorm at hand we were going to have to do some maneuvering. We were different this time around taking it all in stride and making the most of the moment. I was not freaked out by pain.

When I was sure it was time, we gathered the necessity bag and called the Military Police for an escort. It snowed quite a bit and was dreadfully cold. Stephen was born in that snowstorm, a blizzard mind you. He was born by caesarean birth due to complications. We decided not to have more children. The pregnancies were fine, but the deliveries were a problem. This time was more stressful than the first birth, and I became concerned for my health. Each time I told Phillip if I did not make it through childbirth save the child and make sure the baby knew how much his mom loved him; choose the baby if the doctor offered a choice.

I hoped to be like my mom. Though her first birth was caesarean, the last three were natural deliveries. It did not work that way for me. Complications delayed deliveries until surgery was necessary. We told the doctor to do whatever he needed to do. I followed with, "Tie my tubes." The doctor said, "I don't have that paperwork in front of me." As they wheeled me from one room into the operating room, I said, "Get it and tie my tubes." One of the nurses said, "She's going into shock." I said, "I'm not going anywhere until somebody tells me he's tying my tubes." They offered anesthesia, I refused it until I knew a tube ligation would be performed. The doctor began insisting on the paperwork. A nurse ran in with it in her hands, yelling, "I've got it." The doctor advised he saw the paperwork for the procedure. I said okay, started counted backwards, and collapsed only to awaken hours later with a beautiful big baby boy. The patience that doctor showed was commendable. It was obvious he was in control but made me feel I was.

Stephen was beautiful, simply gorgeous, and fat. He weighed nine pounds ten ounces and was an armful. We explained to Phil Jr. that we had a little brother for him. This was his baby too. He was delighted. The next day Phil Jr. held him in his little arms, which was not an easy task because Stephen was large. Phillip supported his head, but Phil Jr. held him with all his strength and little muscles bulging. He kissed him on the forehead and looked up towards his dad for relief from his heavy baby brother. His dad scooped Stephen out of his arms giving relief.

Our time at the guest house expired. Phillip and Phil Jr. had to move out. With a few more days before the scheduled departure date, one of Phillip's friends opened his home to Phillip and Phil Jr. while I finished my extended stay at the hospital. My stitches tore open on the original day of the checkout and lead to an additional seven day stay. The additional week was not planned, and guest housing was no longer available. When I left Irwin Army Hospital, I joined my family at the Jacob's home for a few days as we geared up for the long drive to Georgia with the boys. The frequent stops were necessary as we exited the car for some long stretches and patching up as we changed my bandages and cleaned the wound. The doctor insisted, and we agreed it would be done to ensure my safety and the healing process. We had a toddler and a newborn directing our path as their demands had to be met. We were ridiculously driven.

Phillip and I were glad to be back on the East coast. It was nearer even though it was nine hours away. It was easily drivable compared to Kansas. This location offered more time with family. We visited home often. Phillip was glad he was nearby when his Grandmother Inez passed. His grandmas were his matriarchs, so much a part of his life. Stories of his youth with her, his cousin Wallace, and so many of his other first cousins were hysterical as he shared good times. We were glad for the time she spent with Phil Jr. and Stevie even though Stevie was only a few months old. She loved on them as only grandmas can do as she was a great grandmother. That is just grandma to the second power. The loss was enormous. The loss of his Grandfather Mike also. It was not easy to say goodbye to those who helped mold our lives. I understood how important family was to Phillip. He loved them unquestionably.

While we lived in Atlanta, our families visited from North Carolina quite a bit. It was fantastic. Many could not pop in while we were in Kansas, but returning to the Southeast coast allowed the family an opportunity to travel. A nine-hour drive was much easier for the family. It gave a chance for Phillip to check on his mom after the loss of her mom. We wanted to help her through it not knowing really what to do. We decided to visit her more and bring her with us to Georgia for visits. That was an added blessing as she tolerated the nine hour drive. His dad Mike seemed to be okay. We visited him when we were in town. We checked on our families.

We took advantage of our adventurous nature and became familiar with the city of Atlanta, the Martin Luther King, Jr. historical sites, and neighboring cities. I loved Dr. King from my youth and felt honored to visit his childhood spaces. Phillip felt the same way. There was so much to do in Atlanta. Phillip and I continued our Sunday drives adding Saturday to our exploits. His military missions were different at this duty station. It permitted additional family time. The boys were very young but enjoyed the sites, plays, concerts, and wrestling events. I enjoyed dressing the boys for church in their cute little suits and ties. They were these tiny people with all this personality. We did not attend often, but they looked adorable when visited. We found great friends at this duty station also.

The two years in Georgia passed quickly, far too quickly. We worked full and part time jobs and spent every penny we earned. We saved very little. At twenty-five, I thought I was very smart but realized some choices were not even sensible financial investments. Mommy warned us against credit card debt suggesting one or two cards only even though she had a few. The language of limited cards and usage just did not seem sensible. I heard her talking, but it was so easy to pull the plastic and pay later. That is until we ran into some financial problems. When the cards became a burden I shared it with her, and she said she warned us so that we would not have to go through the feelings of frustration or shame due to overwhelming payments. She explained she had more than one card but used them wisely. She encouraged us to get rid of the extra cards and unnecessary loans so that we would have the freedom of enjoying our paychecks or at least some of it. I listened but did not follow through. Each time the bills arrived, I remembered again.

Before long we were packing for Baumholder, Germany. Our loved ones dreaded the move, but we were excited. We understood Phillip's military obligations might take us further than the Midwest, and we liked the idea though it would cost us family time. We planned to return home once a year as done while living in Kansas. This was an enormous change from seeing family seven or eight times a year for the last two years, but we affectionately explained the call of duty. Of course, the mothers tried to persuade us to leave the boys in North Carolina or Washington, D.C. while Phillip completed his assignment, but it was not the option for us. I was going with him, and so were the boys if the military permitted.

While watching the boys play, I wondered if I would have the same type of connection with them as my mom had with me. Would that intuition kick in? Would I know things that were happening in their lives before they told me? Would they love me as I loved her? Time would answer the questions eventually, so I just decided to enjoy the moments.

While we were in Germany, Teenage Mutant Ninja Turtles came on the scene and the boys loved them. Everything had to have a turtle on it. One of Phillip's younger cousins gifted in art painted two pullovers with turtles on them. The boys loved those pullovers even though they hated to pull clothing over their heads. They did not care when it came to those sweaters. They wanted to wear them year round. Toys were turtles, pajamas had turtles, jackets at least had a turtle patch, and even the bedding had turtles. They wanted turtles everywhere, and we bought them since the cost was nominal. Phil Jr's favorite turtle was Donatello since Phil's middle name was Donnell and Stevie's favorite turtle was Michelangelo since his middle name was Michael. Their characteristics were similar. It was funny that the personalities fit so perfectly.

One day after seeing the movie twice at the theater and several times at home as a rental, Stevie had some questions for me. He talked on and on about the turtles and turtle power. After much discussion, he asked if his middle name was Michael. I said yes. He said, "Then call me Mikey. I no want to be Stevie no more. I'm Mikey like the Ninja Turtle. No Stevie no more, okay Mommy?" I explained that Michael was his middle name. He asked if it were a real name. "Is it me too?" he asked. I assured him it was really his name. Then with certainty he wanted to use Mikey instead of Stevie. He nodded assuring me of his decision.

This three year old amazed me. He requested a turtle pizza party for his friends and a name change. I shared the update with Phillip when he arrived home from work. He laughed and said it was fine. "We just have to inform our relatives of the change," he said. Phillip called Stevie out of his room using his new nickname Mikey. He ran and jumped into his dad's lap smiling as he yelled with gladness. Phil Jr. explained to his dad about the new name and why the change was necessary to the child formerly known as Stevie. Phillip acted as though he heard it for the first time nodding his head with expressions of support. When we phoned relatives for our biweekly check-in, we told them of the name change.

At home in North Carolina, the original Steve had grown up and enlisted in the U.S. Navy. He married his teenage sweetheart Vanessa, had a daughter named Keosha, and was anticipating the birth of his son Stephen Jr. Military life had attracted him too. We were happy for them; however, Mikey was thrilled that another Stephen was on the way. We explained that Steve Jr. was named after Steve just like Phil Jr. and his dad. Mikey asked about Steve as his real first name. We assured him it was, and he assured us the baby's name was because of him too. "He's Steve like me," he said. We laughed at his logic as he showed how it related to him. Phillip liked Mikey's name change since his dad and granddad's name were Mike and his brother Butch named Michael. He was following the tradition.

The lives of our siblings had changed from youth to adulthood. Phillip and I shared stories about our childhood showing the boys pictures from the many photo albums. This kept our family before their eyes. We laughed at the mayhem of our youth. Our boys grew up hearing about our good and bad adventures. They heard about the cornfields, mud pies, favorite pets, and chastisements too, lots of stuff.

They saw pictures of their grandparents, aunts, uncles, and cousins. We talked so much about family until the boys were excited to speak to them and visit. We discussed the changes in our families when Jo and her husband divorced. She moved from home to Elizabeth City. She had a third son named Michael. Of course, Mikey was sure this was because of him too. Denise was in Maryland living the happy single life. She was like Mommy encouraging everybody to enjoy life regardless of the challenges. Stephanie graduated from Elizabeth City State University with plans of being an educator. Butch was working in Philadelphia, PA and visited home often. Steve was sailing all over. Since our parents were no longer married, we did not talk to our dads as often as our moms. Still we stayed connected. We tried to keep up with the happenings by phone calls. Visiting home once a year just did not seem like enough time with the folks we loved so dearly. The boys fell in love with them regardless to how far apart we lived. We shared stories about our friends reminding them of their little friendships established from state to state and country to country.

Germany was fun for many reasons. Phillip was stationed at Baumholder; we lived on the hillside of Strassburg Kaserne in Idar-Oberstein, Germany. It was beautiful. From our balcony, we saw winding streets that opened up to the city below; on the left stood a castle embedded in rocks and imposing landscape. Our view was breathtaking. The streets were narrow and curved around the mountainous rocks and hills. Simply beautiful.

It snowed a great deal, and the boys loved playing outside regularly. They had many friends in the apartment complex occupied by military families. Some of their playmates were German children since a German and a French Kaserne neighbored our building. They communicated the best they knew, and each began to teach the other his language until the boys spoke conversational German and English. We practiced speaking German in the department stores. The nationals seemed very patient as I blundered of their language many times while finding the correct pronunciation. They smiled appreciating the effort. The military gave a few German language classes for the family members to educate us on the customs, culture, and the basics. I took advantage of those classes, but it still required a lot of practice. I tried not to frustrate the nationals in my attempts to speak the language as I shopped throughout the villages.

We walked a lot as was the custom of the Germans. Phillip ran up and down the slopes and Phil Jr. tried to run in his steps as Mikey and I trailed behind them. I pushed the stroller knowing the boys would get tired of running eventually. The boys enjoyed racing their dad on foot. Often stopping the car as the sites demanded we toured castles and cathedrals on our Sunday drives. After a long walk, the drive home was a time of rest for the boys as they napped exhausted from their journey.

Phillip was away because of military exercises again. Kansas had taught me to make the most of our time, but occasionally my plans seemed more significant to me than the training mission. It sounded foolish when I said it aloud, but it just seemed to me the training could happen at other times. Phillip said he wanted to be home, but things happened in the world regardless to the important happenings of our lives. We had to be willing to sacrifice so that our country could stay safe and prepared. He was a soldier at heart, but I was thinking about the birthdays he would miss. He said he would miss them so that his sons could be safe for other birthdays. I knew his philosophy and grew accustomed to it though displeased sometimes, and now the boys were old enough to notice the absences. He often called them near placing each on a knee to explain the purpose of what he was doing. He was away most birthdays, some holidays and anniversaries. I did not argue at length. There was no purpose to that. It did not change the fact that he had to do what was required, and I did not want to make him feel bad about things he could not control. We knew this would happen again. It was military life, and we chose it.

On the Fourth of July and other holidays there were activities provided by the military morale welfare and recreation department. Phillip's unit was on an exercise two of the three Independence Day holidays while we were in Germany, but the children and I mingled with other families during the holidays. Our friends and their children gathered as we proceeded to the activities and firework displays. We learned to make the most of the situation. We could not dwell on our spouses' absences, so we celebrated the holidays and birthdays while our husbands were away and then again when they returned. The children were happy to celebrate twice.

Our travels had already taken us many places outside Phillip's duty stations. We visited Dodge City and the like while we were in Kansas, Helen and the Callaway Gardens in Georgia, France and Czech while in Germany and many other places. We saw castles and ruins, salt mines and buffalo. Yet our hearts were at home with our folks. We enjoyed every location as well as the culture and the people, but there was no place like home.

I spoke with Mommy weekly sometimes longing for our conversations on the front porch simply sharing everyday life. We sent little keepsakes from the different places. Nothing compared to the intimate conversations that kept me out of trouble. Mommy was glad for our exploits and proud that we were not inhibited by the fear of flight or people, places or things. She was especially glad that Phillip was a swimmer and kept the boys in the water. She was afraid to swim since she almost drowned as a teenager. She was so concerned for our safety and avoidance of water until she passed that fear on to her girls even though Phillip tried to rid me of that phobia.

Mommy, Jean, and the family were missed at holiday meals as I prepared our favorites. Most holidays Phillip and I were away from our folks except the Georgia assignment. We sent pictures and wrote letters, but it was not the same. Nevertheless, we made it work. The telephone proved to be a great source of comfort as we connected. I lost touch with my high school friends, college friends, and friends from the different duty stations, but I was not going to lose touch with my family. Every now and then I connected with friends from the past. Thank goodness we had some photographs and plenty memories. I shared stories with the boys about the life of their mom and dad from childhood through adulthood. I just wish I had stayed in touch with everyone.

Monica was pretty good about that. She was one of the members of the young wives club as I have recently named us. She stayed connected calling from time to time, regardless to the state or country we lived. She kept us linked with some of our friends by way of updates. I was always glad to hear from her and hear that everyone was doing well. We were stationed all over the map. Some families were no longer in the military. I was just glad to hear they were okay.

Sometimes being homesick was inevitable while Phillip was away on maneuvers. I talked to family a bit more frequent when he was away. Work and children kept me busy and longing. Military family life was not for the intolerant or faint of heart. We had to be flexible.

Although Phillip missed first steps, birthdays, first words and even first crushes, the boys did not get angry with their dad. Well there was one incident, which Phillip had a 30-day training while we were in Atlanta. Mikey (then Stevie) was almost two and pretty angry at Phillip for being gone so long. Thirty days were a long time in the life of a two-year old. Mikey was mad for probably an hour before he was back sitting on his dad's lap and trying to play games with him. I kept telling the boys their dad would be back soon. I guess soon was not soon enough for him. We did not let Phillip's absences stand in the way of keeping him abreast of missed events. We caught him up giving as much detail as possible about the happenings when he returned.

Phil Jr's first crush was on a six year old military dependent named Candace whose parents were both soldiers. Phil was five and enamored with this little girl. She could do no wrong especially in Phil's eyes. They played together in the sandbox with the rest of the children. He asked me a question that she had already answered. He said, "Mom Candace knows 'cause she's six. She's a wo-man." Six and already a woman. I guess that made him a little man. His little face revealed the seriousness of his conviction. It was funny although he was serious about his point. I told his dad, and we shared a private chuckle of course not around Phil Jr.

Life changes can be swift for the military family. There was talk of war in the Middle East in January of 1991 shortly after the first of the year, and we were listening. The talk became a reality as our families were temporarily dismantled. Troops from our neighborhood asked friends and neighbors to keep an eye on their spouses and children left behind. Phillip gathered our boys to tell them he was leaving. The boys nodded in agreement as their dad talked of patriotism and what that meant for them. They did not want him to go, but they were proud of the military helping others and keeping America safe especially where our family lived stateside. Phillip's brother Steve was at sea with the Navy. We watched the news for updates.

Families pulled together. Stateside calls were frequent. I joined many other family members who watched and waited for acceptable news while sitting in front of the television. We wondered how long it would take the mission as we prayed there would not be casualties. In the evenings, some of us gathered to boost morale. It was a way of checking on each other. We watched movies and reflected on better times as we took moments from our frustrations.

One Saturday morning while the boys were playing in their bedroom, Phil Jr. came in the living room where I was seated. He was troubled. I was watching the news but turned it off when he entered to keep the information from him and give my full attention. His question took me by surprise. He asked, "Mommy, are we divorced from Daddy? Where's my Daddy?" Positioning my face directly in front of his face, I let go of the shock of his inquiry and said, "No, Baby. We are not divorced. Daddy is away helping in the war. Remember he had talked to you and Mikey before he left, and your friend Chris' dad is away too, and your friend Julian's dad is away. Almost everybody's dad in our apartment building is gone. That's where your dad is. We are not divorced. Okay?" As I listed at least five of his friends' dads by name, he remembered they were away from their families also. He nodded satisfied with my answer and went back in the room to finish playing. Phillip was not in Kuwait. He was in another location supporting the mission.

I shook my head realizing its impact on the children. Maybe I was shielding them too much, but it was necessary. The news was too graphic. The children wanted to know when their dad was returning, and I did not have the answer. I responded, "Soon." I did not want to speculate because I certainly did not know. I was surprised that Phil Jr. thought of divorce. He was only five years old, and he never heard his father, and I talk about divorce. We argued very little in front of them, yet Phil Jr. figured it had to be a possibility. He seemed satisfied with the reassurance. Each day I functioned as though everything was okay. It was not. Every day brought anxieties. Thank God for employment; this took my focus for a moment.

I was employed with the Army Education Center at the Miesau Army Depot where the students were ninety-five percent military personnel.

It was a joy teaching. The classroom size increased to sometimes greater than twenty students while other times possibly as little as three to five students. Class size depended on the troop's mission and availability. It dwindled to zero military and one civilian from a full class. A knock at the classroom door ensured this as a messenger requested one or more of the soldiers report to the unit. The soldiers moved swiftly as we bid a temporary farewell and hope of a speedy return. The class decreased until there was only one student, a military spouse who had just received word she was pregnant after years of trying. That was great news, but her husband deployed for the war right after he got the news of her pregnancy. Desert Shield/Desert Storm had not bypassed Miesau. I prayed it would end, and the soldiers come back from deployment quickly and unharmed. The thought of war was scary and though their faces were brave I was very concerned for them.

At home, I played with the boys and tried to continue as usual. Their dad had been away many times. I tried to give the sense that this was just like any other time. But this was far from the truth. We had a war on our hands, and I was uneasy. I did not want to share this fear with the other wives and make them more uneasy. They had their own fears to battle. Normalcy was the only way to offer some solace while attempting to make the boys feel as secure as possible and not worry them. It was a challenge to protect their childhood. Although a very different state of affairs, there were some similarities to the privacy and peace my mom tried to create for us while my parents tried to figure out their lives. Like her, I wanted to shield and protect my children as well as avoid questions that would create even more anxiety. It was not an easy task because I wholeheartedly believed truth trumped deception. Nevertheless, I hid it from the boys giving it in very small measures watered down with a lot of hope and conjecture.

Two friends from work shared their faith in God with me. I did not ask questions or request their insight; yet, they offered vulnerability as we glimpsed their lives. They were focused on sharing hope and the significance of faith. I understood what they were saying, but I did not want to hear it at the time. I was uncomfortable since I was not attending church, reading the Bible, or following traditional religious behavior. They did not talk about my lifestyle or offer slurs. Still I realized I could be a better person in some areas. They assured me it was not about showing good church behavior, it was all heart. I felt convicted though they did not talk about me. They shared their imperfections, and I saw my own. They shared of how God's love was rich, honest, and pure. He was not condemning, but loving. After a while, I started listening and asking questions. They seemed to have a handle on their belief. While I was fretting, they seemed at peace about things. One friend had just received notice from her husband that he was deploying to Kuwait. She was still calm. Somewhere in those conversations I began to reconnect with my own faith. They were not trying to make me believe in God. I already believed. They wanted to remind me of the truth and share comfort in the midst of the difficult times. I really needed that. I was still worried about my family, friends, and the war. The ladies did not back down. They were determined to encourage me so that I could encourage others and my family.

On my daily hour drive to work, I started praying regularly, even while at work. I took advantage of my lunch break to walk to the nearby chapel desiring a little privacy. The installation chaplain was inside the sanctuary. After greeting and inquiring if I needed assistance, he departed as I smiled assuring him I was okay. I was not okay, but I did not want to admit it to him or to myself. I was worried about the war and the troops. I saw faces as they got the news to report for the new assignment. War meant casualties. I wanted another solution. These were my friends. Some of my students were female soldiers. They were single, married, and some had children. I did not want anything tragic to happen, and this troubled me. I did not have answers.

Sitting down on one of the church bench near the middle of the sanctuary, I began to cry. I hoped Phillip's assignment would not change and require him near the battle. I thought of military friends, spouses, children, and the stateside families. I wondered if the world knew the sacrifices these brave men and women made. I wanted the troops to know they were appreciated. I thought of Phillip and his sons. I could not stop crying. My allegiance belonged to America. The price for freedom was high; nevertheless, I was in the company of those willing to pay the price. It was bravery, loyalty to country, duty and so much more. I had to pray for all of them. That was my duty at that moment. I was sure of it. I kept praying for the troops and the civilians that were in harm's way. I left feeling as though I had helped a little.

My faith continued to grow, and peace became a part of my life in a way that I never expected. Another day while praying in the chapel, there was such an overpowering peace. I turned around verifying that I was alone in the chapel. I was alone, yet I knew with every fiber of my being that I was not alone. I knew it was the peace of God, and it was indescribable and intoxicating. It was a sensation yet more. I could not explain. I was overwhelmed.

Acknowledging my imperfections I realized I missed this relationship with God, the one greater than myself, the Creator of all life, and he loved me. I had never felt more connected with him than at that moment. I asked God for forgiveness and began forgiving others. Some stuff had hooked on to my little red wagon along life's journey to adulthood. It did not just tag along. I put it in the wagon. Some issues became permanent fixtures as I carried them so long. I was ashamed that I had held on to some concerns so long, but since no one asked for forgiveness, it had not been given. In the past, I felt no remorse for that. Now I was starting to let go of the hurts.

Life became less scary. It was good news. There would be plenty of mistakes in the future, but I was committed and submitted to this endless love. I sat there basking a while longer merely swept away. Rededicating my life to Christ was amazing. I did not go to the chapel with this intent, but felt so much better than when I entered the sanctuary. I was ready to go back to work.

When the ladies who shared their faith heard of my experience they were thrilled. Shortly afterwards, they received job promotions and relocated to other areas of the country but stayed in touch. Mommy and Jean were ecstatic as I shared the news. Not many weeks later, Phillip returned, and the war was over. All of our friends were headed home. We were so thankful it ended and very sad for the casualties. Our friends made it back, but not everyone was as fortunate. Some families bore the greatest loss. Our prayers were with them all.

THE OTHER STORMS

At the end of Desert Storm, all of our neighbors-soldiers returned home. Excited with anticipation we received the news of their arrivals. They had many stories to share and even more to keep tucked away. We were just so glad to see them, touch them, and hear their voices.

Amidst our gladness, we received a call from home with the news of Ma-Ma's death. I was floored. We flew home for the funeral while the rest of our friends were flying back to their families from the war. I desired to see my friends, but had to go. I packed up the children for a short stateside visit; the military permitted Phillip to accompany the children and me. Her death was a surprise even though she was ninety-six years old. She always looked the same to me.

She was in relatively good health. I made a point of seeing her whenever home allowing the boys to spend time with her too. She still had her sense of humor calling me her clown. Whenever my sisters and I were home, we contacted each other so that we could visit her together. Even visiting the area solo did not dissuade a visit to see Ma-Ma. She was our heart. I wanted her to laugh, and her eyes sparkle. As she laughed, I clowned even more. I phoned her while she was at home, but when she moved to a nursing home, only twice in six months. Whenever I spoke with Niece and Jo, she was mentioned in our conversation. It was not the same as speaking to her. I spoke to someone at the facility who assured me she was fine though she was resting and unavailable to take a call. Most assuredly I knew I would see her in a few months when we returned home for a visit. I never imagined life without her. I knew where I could find her.

When we arrived stateside the family was waiting at the airport. Daddy was doing as well as expected to endure his great loss. His mom was iconic to him, to all of us. She belonged to all of us, but especially him. He had a great love for her. They had a special connection. My mom offered him condolence. It was a loss to her also. By now the two of them had rediscovered many kind words towards one another and had forgiven the past. We mourned our loss together.

Niece, Jo with her children, and Mommy gathered as we remembered. A bystander, overhearing the reason for the reunion, joined our conversation uninvited. She noted it unusual, and a great sacrifice to travel from Germany for a grandmother's funeral. I shared that we were a close family, and our grandmother was an intricate part of our lives. She said she would not have done it. I was amazed that she joined our conversation contributing that the sacrifice was too costly when she did not know us. As the lady walked away, I turned to the family and explained how offended I was at her comment. Mommy reminded me that the lady was speaking about her own life not mine. Maybe she was attempting to compliment the sacrifice; nevertheless, it was the opinion of a stranger. I said okay and focused on the family as we had not been together in quite a while. I held my composure realizing maybe she meant no harm with her intrusion.

It was difficult to leave the family. We recalled our childhood, when we were good and misbehaved. We remembered Ma-Ma's hum while she baked. We remembered family. Tears, laughter, and hugs flooded as we parted again with our lives in different places. We left North Carolina headed to Germany after being at home a couple of weeks with family, and we said goodbye to Ma-Ma. One thing was sure, life and death continued its course whether we were home with loved ones or in far away lands.

When we returned to Germany, our friends and neighbors made sure there was little time to grieve, and plenty of celebrating life. The war was really over! The boys played with their friends at the playground. The grown-ups had fun too laughing, playing cards and dominoes, enjoying a wonderfully mild summer. Everybody was glad to be back together again. Stories unfolded about some of the things encountered while in war. The male and female soldiers were mission driven. They said they understood the sacrifice and did what they had to do. It was not comfortable, but they did it. Those of us in the rear shared how we were praying for them and watching the news sometimes glued to the television hoping for the best. The children were happy to have them home too. It was celebration time. Life returned to the familiar.

After a thirty-three month tour, it was time to leave Germany. We enjoyed the tour, but there was a yearning to get back home with the family for a little while. We buried Ma-Ma a year and a half earlier, and I was still longing. We understood home had been many places by now, but home base was still North Carolina. This time we were not going to another military installation; we were going home. Phillip was leaving the military due to an injury. He wanted to stay in service, but that was no longer an option as his body disagreed with his mind, and the cold climate did not help. One thing happened often with military life, hellos and goodbyes. We were accustomed to establishing good relations and in a year, more or less sometimes, bidding farewell though we had become inseparable for a season. It was a part of military life.

We had to decide where to live. Though I was still in love with Atlanta, I did not want to go quite so far from family after living away from them for almost nine years. We decided to live somewhere near home. This would give plenty of time to spend with family and give the boys time to rediscover their grandparents and other relatives. They could really get to know the folks they heard such exciting stories about while living abroad. First thing was first. We had to prepare to leave another home away from home. Packing memories and bidding farewell to old and new friendships was just part of the process. This included shopping buddies, Miesau friends, and those in the communities of Baumholder, Heidelberg, and Strassburg.

As we took one of our final drives along the mountainous roadside of Idar-Oberstein and throughout Germany, Phillip and I explained to the boys why we were leaving our home and friends. This was their first recognizable move. Phil Jr. was almost two and Mikey two weeks old when we left Kansas. He was almost four and Mikey two years old when we left Georgia. Previously they were too young to care. Phillip explained why their friends Chris, Candace, and BJ were already gone with their parents to other duty stations. We might see them again one day. After all, the last time he saw his friend Brandon was at Fort Riley, Kansas as a baby so young neither of them remembered the encounters. Now he was in Manheim, Germany and he spent many weekends with the boys growing up together for a little while. Life was like that. He assured them we could stay in touch. It was as simple as explaining the military experience. It was time to go stateside and see our family. They agreed with a definite yes as they cheered at the idea. They wanted to see their grandmas. We smiled and agreed. I thought about the ones they would not see anymore and felt sad. There was no time for that with all the packing ahead.

Relocating back to the United States was not challenging. Many of our closest friends from Germany had left already. It was our turn, and it seemed the perfect time. It was winter, and the cold weather in Carolina was easily adaptable. The weather in Germany was very cold. I would miss the girl-trips taken most anytime with Michelle and Tanya. We shopped whenever we were lost on the winding roads of Saarbrucken. We explored the locale. We were not afraid of being lost. Matter-of-fact, my philosophy paid off in wonderful little treasures throughout our shopping exploits. It only said make the most of the trip as long as you have money or gas. It was time to leave the ladies behind as we journeyed home. They understood since both were military wives. Their husbands were scheduled to relocate stateside soon.

We arrived home a few weeks later, this time without another duty station assignment. Phillip ended his military career. It was exciting while it lasted, but now we were back at home in North Carolina visiting family. We decided to live in Virginia Beach, Virginia. It was an hour drive to Jean or JoAnn's house, and a three hour drive to Denise or Mommy. We had not selected a house, but at least we had a location. By now, Steve and Vanessa had settled in Virginia while Butch was in Pennsylvania, and Stephanie in Maryland. Everyone could be reached within a few hours, even our dads whom we saw less often than our moms. We did not move to Virginia immediately. We stayed with Jean for two months simply reacquainting the boys with family while we found an apartment that was nice and affordable. We wanted a good school district with surrounding entertainment and restaurant venues. It did not matter whether an apartment or a house. We were more concerned with the neighborhood and schools that would best suit the boys and our budget.

Two months passed quickly as we spent time visiting family along the east coast. The boys bonded instantly with family. The photo albums and constant stories helped them identify many relatives. This was so valuable to Phillip and me because we traveled many places, spending only a few weeks here and there with our loved ones. We did not regret it, but it meant the children did not have the opportunity to know their family very well. They still loved them even from a distance, but they did not know them. Those photographs proved to be very important; reminiscing and funny stories made the boys eager to spend time with them.

The first part of settling in was easy as we returned home. It was only a matter of reestablishing contacts with family and getting acclimated to the time zone. Germany was six hours ahead of North Carolina. So much had happened and we had not visited home since Ma-Ma's funeral. It was good to be home and see parents, siblings, all of the immediate family. We also caught a glimpse of some old friends. It was just good to be home again.

It was good to see Mommy. She had not been feeling great lately. She was diabetic. It was not a new condition. She was diagnosed during pregnancy with JoAnn. This condition disappeared after the birth but resurfaced a few years later. There was also a battle with elevated blood pressure, and she had a heart murmur which she insisted was no problem at all. I did not find out about the murmur until my adulthood. The family doctor maintained that stress and diet were the cause of the high blood pressure and diabetes. Assigned insulin injections and medication, she faithfully monitored her levels for years to ensure problems did not arise.

Her strength weakened due to a cold that stubbornly refused to disappear and unable to identify the cause, she visited her doctor. After many tests, she was diagnosed with breast cancer. She was fifty-two and never had a mammogram. She was so careful with diabetes and figured her continued checkups would identify any other problem. Hearing this diagnosis frightened her as well as the rest of us. She remembered her sister Mary died at fifty-one of breast cancer. Mommy decided to fight. She redirected her energies drawing from her faith in God, love of family, and life.

Immediately as family became aware of the diagnosis the calls came. Some were not satisfied with the telephone voice assuring them she was going to be okay. They visited from New York and North Carolina. They also came from various other parts of the east coast. They assured her they would stay in touch. She was not in this fight alone.

She felt love surrounding and comforting her. She declared that love from God and family propelled her to new heights daily as she received calls assuring her that she was not quarantined or isolated from others because of cancer. First cousins, second cousins, third cousins, fourth cousins, cousins once removed and twice loved…it did not matter. They came. It ministered to Denise, Jo, and me. We saw this compassion when we were children as they gathered encouraging each other for whatever battle was before them as well as coming together just because they loved each other and wanted to stay in touch. It showed up for weddings, or when marriages fell apart or children were trespassing on parental authority or someone was sick or died. This love was still alive and poured on Mommy. She needed every bit of it too. Though drained by chemotherapy and loss of appetite each day she strengthened herself and insisted, in spite of it all, she was okay.

We watched her closely to make sure this was true. I was befuddled with news about someone who gave so much and requested so little. Why was she going through this in the first place? Where did cancer come from invading her body and her sister? I stared when she was not looking. I needed confirmation that she was really strong, not simply giving words to comfort us. She truly was okay even though sometimes she had more strength on Thursday than on Monday or vice versa. She refused to complain; therefore, neither would we. It did not matter what we thought about the situation, she needed positive people around her. Denise, JoAnn, Phillip, and I decided we would stay positive and believe with Mommy for her miracle.

Mommy moved in with Denise. While in Maryland, we did whatever we knew made her smile or laugh. And when she did not feel like doing either, we sat surrounding her with the grandchildren— five grandsons. We were quiet when silence was requested calming the energetic boys who settled easily when they heard it was what grandma wanted from them. We broke very few of Denise's knickknacks as I clumsily redirected the boys from the glass items. Denise said let the children play in the room she set up for them because I was not helping protect her things. Meanwhile, Mommy gave multiple hugs as they asked how she felt from day to day. We explained Mommy's condition to the children ranging from ages eight to two with the best words we had for the occasion. They seemed to understand. This eased our minds since we did not have to explain it constantly. They simply got it.

Denise provided the care she recognized she needed. Stephanie graduated from Elizabeth City State University in N.C. and was teaching Early Childhood Education in Maryland, about forty-five minutes away. She visited Mommy and Denise quite often helping as needed. So did our cousin Darnley, who actually was our paternal cousin. Some of our dad's relatives in Maryland visited Mommy and telephoned her which was much appreciated. Her church family regularly popped in to lift her spirits after getting an okay from Denise. Mommy said it always made her feel better even when it was a chore to get dressed to greet visitors.

It was good to hear of the visits. When Jo and I talked to Denise using the three-way phone service she gave updates. Jo was living in Elizabeth City, N.C. while I was staying in Eure, N.C. We each had a four-hour drive to Maryland alternating weekends with both families together at least once a month. This changed from the initial visits of both families coming each weekend with all of the grand boys. We decided to change it because Mommy tried to entertain them and it required too much to be the person she was before the medications. Jo and I watched Denise also to ensure she was not extremely overwhelmed in the everyday battle. She continued working. We realized the pressure she endured seeing our mom frail. It was a lot to ask, but she was willing to make that sacrifice for Mommy. We wanted to be there for the both of them as often as possible regardless to our costs. This was our mom.

Cards flooded the small mail slot opening in the door at the entrance way of Denise's apartment. Get well cards gave Mommy visuals to hold and read over and over. She read the personal handwritten sentiments repeatedly placing them on the table in front of her as she rested on the sofa. She loved cards. Opening them brought smiles even when she only found a signature inside. This helped her on a good day or a not so good day.

Denise, Jo, Phillip, and I talked about praying for a full recovery. We could not consider the other option. Technology had increased since our Aunt Mary's battle, and though a cure had not been found in the fourteen years since our aunt's diagnosis, methods of fighting the disease offered greater success than formerly. The treatment was going well, and Mommy said her oncologist said whatever she was doing continue because it was bringing her great results. That was good news. It was necessary to have a positive and stress free environment while she healed.

Jo had two school-aged sons; still, she brought them with her on every trip. She stayed at Mommy's side. Her children accompanied her as the holiday season provided more time away from work and school. It was not easy, but she made it work. Denise never complained, not even once. She worked at the mental institution in Washington, D.C., we knew she was exhausted when she ended those long hours and came home, but she insisted she was okay. When we arrived at her house she still tried to play the hostess, but we sat her down while we cooked and cleaned for those few days. We supported each other emotionally and financially as much as possible.

We needed to be okay while we helped our mom. She still had her mother antennas which would identify something was amiss with her children. We understood that sometimes you do not get a second chance to do what you earnestly wanted to do the first time. We needed each other. Our faith offered strength and courage when I could not get advice from my oldest and dearest confidant. Phillip never complained about the travel or the cost.

Shortly after moving back stateside we enrolled six-year-old Phil Jr. in the local school system where Jean lived while we stayed with her. We did not want him to miss school while we selected a home, and it seemed pretty definite Eure, NC was home until Mommy was better. When we returned stateside we were all unaware of a sickness with Mommy. She was unaware also.

Phillip's mom kept the children whenever they were not with us in Maryland. She rode with us on occasion to visit her old friend even though long trips were not her favorite. She made up her mind to do it and just did. Other times they spoke on the phone. Phillip's brother Butch drove to District Heights from Philadelphia almost every time we visited after he heard Mommy was ill. Somehow we dropped the ball initially and did not tell him. We had not called or heard from him as he was away on a project for work. When he received the news weeks later, he came to Maryland. Surrounded by young folks cheering her victory, Mommy wanted all of the grandsons with her. Regardless to our opinion of what she needed, she knew she wanted to see all of the boys as often as possible. So we brought them and tried not to let them tire her out too much respectfully. Stephanie visited often, and Darnley too. Steve and Vanessa visited also though they were expecting their third child, baby girl Kendra. Vanessa rode the distance to support and keep morale high. We were the same family in North Carolina, Kansas, Georgia, Maryland or wherever.

When everyone visited we gathered at Denise's apartment and made pallets on the floor. We just wanted to be together and be with Mommy. No one complained about the sleeping arrangements. It seemed natural. It was the only way to be together and make the most of our time. We were used to making adjustments. As children when family visited there were no hotels in our hometown; therefore, we knew how to adapt. We made pallets. As young adults, it was elementary. No one wanted a hotel room. We simply hung out together.

We stayed with Mommy and Denise for the weekends talking, watching movies, laughing, playing games, and just having fun. She loved it. She loved laughter and joined us. There were no sad movies or conversation. The air was lively changing television channels as needed because there was always a sad story on the television. Scooby Doo, Charlie Brown, and Dennis the Menace were still her favorites. As long and often as necessary, we were together until Mommy returned to good health. I could not imagine my children oblivious to her. I could not imagine life without her. She was too important to dismiss because of our busy lives. She belonged to us, and we belonged to her. We had to do all we could do. She had to know that we wanted her well again because we loved her.

Early mornings before the group emerged I read the Bible to her, and we talked about the passages and how she saw herself in them. She shared some of lessons life had taught her and mistakes were human nature. Forgiveness was the key to forward movement. She had not always been so forgiving but always willing to try. I simply did not want to let folks off the hook. She assured me I had victim mentality, and I had to be the victor. I was twenty-eight, but she said it was a lesson to learn and not delay. She shared how proud she was of her family with all our imperfections. Those were great talks while everyone else slept. I knew it was our time as we looked around the room. Loved ones were asleep all around us. We laughed at some of their sleeping positions and expressions as I mimicked them. Her laughter was returning.

Early one morning, I found Mommy already up and ready for the day. Smiling and excited I walked over, sat down on the sofa very close to her, and laid my head on her shoulder. She started talking about unconditional love as though I really needed this pounded in my head. I did not mind because she was sharing what she learned and how important time should be to everyone. I listened hearing her words and thanked God for having her still with me. I wanted to cry about her afflictions, but there was no time for that. I concealed the tears as I held on to her arm nestling on her shoulder. Afterwards, it was time to prepare breakfast for the bunch and she wanted to do it. I was glad to help. Phil Jr. and Terence Jr. awoke energized. We quieted them and sent them off to wash up. They were ready to serve.

Usually on the weekends Mommy's cousins from the north and south came to visit. There were no somber visits. They laughed like old times as they continued to reminisce about the days of old. We even met some of her cousins for the first time. They heard she was sick and wanted to stop by and wish her well. Mommy knew them, but we did not. They brought cards from other cousins unable to be there. It was incredible. They refused to stay away.

As Mommy's energy returned she started to move around more and even cook a meal now and again. It was therapy for her, going to church also. She no longer had her flowers to work out her frustrations or to use as her thinking pots. The house plants looked good though. The greatest change was the loss of hair. Although she weighed less than previous, the hair was what she called her glory. It was gone. We told her how beautiful she was without the wigs as she adjusted them onto of her smooth head. In the absence of hair, she was still very beautiful; she was alive and getting well. That was beautiful right by itself.

As Mommy gained her strength, she showed hospitality to everyone who entered the door. She let everyone know how much she appreciated their prayers. She was thankful to God for the love she felt from so many people. She said so on many occasions. We assured her it was because of her uniqueness, but she disagreed. She said it was God's love, and it was the same feeling he wanted everyone to know. She appreciated everyone who gave anything; she thanked those she did not see that prayed for her. She said she knew some folks were praying. She reminded us to show that same kind of compassion to others. She felt it was necessary for the mind, body, and spirit. She had a new appreciation for life. It felt like I was back on the front porch talking with her and getting a lesson in 'love your fellowman.' The old Yvonne Brown was getting her groove again, and we were thrilled. She would not let us forget to be thankful. She was glad to get back to her church choir, and the rest of her life.

THE WINDS OF CHANGE

I learned through this ordeal that cancer was not as powerful as I believed. It was such a dreaded disease that I never thought of people surviving it, and now it had attacked Mommy. I did not know how to fight except with faith, but cancer could not win. It personally touched some of those who came to encourage her and some had lost loved ones, but they did not suggest the worst to her. Instead, they offered hope and optimism. They offered it, and we took it. Hope was the key to enjoying life. We were willing to share her with others while we enjoyed the day.

Initially, the thought of cancer gave so much fear that I did not know how to process it in the life of my mother. I had to find the strength to believe in better days ahead and hope for a woman that had given encouragement to so many others. She needed strength instead of the daily reminder of the disease she was fighting. She was truly getting better.

Later our lives returned to the familiar. Mommy was okay. Now it was time to find a home in Virginia Beach, Virginia. We moved into a three-bedroom townhouse and unpacked containers of stored household goods. The movers unloaded as we began putting everything in its place. Our brothers, sisters, and moms joined us unpacking the many boxes. At last we were settling into civilian life again. It seemed a little strange though. The military had been our lives since before we had children. I missed the uniforms, troops, and the atmosphere. Much happened in the couple of months since we left Germany. I knew home was where we were needed, but I missed military life.

It did not take the boys long to get in the swing of being with family. Quickly they were hiding behind aunts, uncles, and grandmas when they were in trouble. They knew as long as there was at least one grandmother around, they would not get the punishment we wanted for them. Mommy and Jean visited us in Virginia at the same time. I do not know who enjoyed it more, Phillip and me, the moms, or the children. These moms cooked our favorite meals collaborating menus and cleaning everything in their paths. They insisted on helping with the chores pampering while they stayed. I refused at first because that was not why we wanted them to visit, but gave in as they did it anyway. I did not feel threatened in my role as the woman of the house. It seemed so natural having both of them in the house with us. Both of them loved us; they did not take over, but made it impossible to say no to good home cooked meals with the flavors of our youth saturating the house. Their sense of humor coupled with the children's antics kept the house full of laughter. We wanted them to stay permanently, but they said no.

Our moms stayed as long as they wanted before returning to their homes. It was usually two weeks each time, but they were welcome to stay longer. Together we shopped, dined, watched movies, took evening drives, and simply relaxed in each other's company. Since the Bible was a practical part of our lives by now, we studied it together. This was usually late in the afternoon or early evening before dinner or directly afterwards. There were no in-law feuds.

We saw Mike, Phillip's dad, quite often. He treated me very well, always considerate of my presence when I accompanied Phillip. He was always willing to help us; we appreciated it and always repaid the debt. I really liked the connection I saw between Phillip and his dad.

Grandparents were an important staple for our family. Grandma Inez (Jean's mom) and Grandma Hattie (Mike's mom) made me feel a part of the family long before Phillip and I walked the aisle of matrimony. They welcomed me in their homes and never made me feel like a guest. I was instantly family even though Phillip and I were just dating. I felt at home with them and told my mom. She was pleased and reminded me of my upbringing. Be mindful of your manners in someone else's home. Phillip shared great stories about his grandparents. I shared stories also as Phillip spent time with Ma-Ma whenever I visited her.

He had met her before he met me actually. Jean said Ma-Ma was the midwife who delivered Phillip. That surprised both him and me.

Prompted by overseas employment opportunities, Phillip considered working in Kuwait. He applied for local jobs but was not hired. With almost nine years of military experience, a wife, and two young sons, he decided it was a time for action. He took the job. We talked about it at length and decided it would work. This time Phillip would work as a civilian on a military installation, and he would be unaccompanied by family. He could work, save, and come home.

We separated in the past, but the missions only lasted six to ten weeks at the most excluding finishing college, joining the military, the military exercise in Germany, and the Gulf War. That being stated, there were times we were apart. We lived through them.

We traveled the globe together. The one-year contract in Kuwait would help repair damages sustained from the Gulf War. We knew it was a worthwhile project; nevertheless, leaving the family was not an easy decision. I struggled with it even though it seemed to be the only offer at the moment. We waited ample time to find something else, but nothing else seemed to be happening, and our savings had dwindled. I suggested working again since I enjoyed it and it would help the family, but Phillip insisted it was his responsibility to provide for the family. I did not take it as a macho thing, although to some degree it was, but I knew what he meant.

Family helped with the transition of Phillip leaving for overseas employment; the local church was a great support too. By now the boys were seven and five years old. They understood that their father was going to help the war people rebuild their lives. Phillip bought two small globes that displayed all countries including Saudi Arabia, Kuwait, and Iraq. He pointed to Kuwait and said this was where he would be for a little while. They practiced finding it on the map and spelling it. They were not happy about their dad leaving because they remembered the Gulf War. At first I did not think the globes helped. Later they showed no anxiety as the globes were cushioned cloth balls. They tossed them around quite a bit. We showed them all of the places we lived. They made a game of trying to catch it on one of the locations. After a while, they played dodge ball before we reminded them it was a globe. Hearing the news reports scared them and they did not like separating from their dad for the war again. After many questions and sad faces, they accepted their latest challenge…to watch out for mom while he was away.

Phillip was missed. We talked often via telephone, but it was very expensive. I literally screamed one day as I opened an $880.00 phone bill. I wanted to faint. Instead, I called him to talk about the excessive cost of staying in touch. I could have been smarter, but at that moment I was not. We talked about the waste and how we had to find a more economical way of staying in touch before laughing about being on the phone. We had to be smarter and not let emotions lead us. After a while, we decided to use the Internet, though it did not offer the common touch. Handwritten letters passed between the continents as we affirmed our connection. The boys wrote letters and drew pictures to share their day with him.

Those expensive phone bills had to stop. Mommy suggested brief conversations, but I was not very good at that. Words rolled off my tongue catching Phillip up on everything he missed. I had to change. It was not easy, but every time I wanted to do it my way I thought about those $500.00 and $600.00 phone bills. Mommy and Jean suggested it was cheaper to visit Kuwait, although they did not want me to consider it. At almost $900.00, they said stop talking a couple of months and just buy a ticket to talk for a few weeks while you visit him.

Mommy visited Virginia Beach and visited JoAnn also. We gladly shared her taking turns with her one or two week stays. Traveling from daughter to daughter, she considered leaving the Washington, D.C. area and returning to Belvidere, North Carolina to be near her sister and brother. It did not matter to us. We just wanted her to be happy. Every time she traveled home she visited her sister. The two would travel to visit their brother who was still institutionalized. She never gave up hope that he would regain his mental faculties and live at home again. Sometimes he recognized them and other times he did not. It was a strain to see him there, but she said she had to see her brother regardless to where he was staying. She wanted him to know he was loved and not forgotten. She called him constantly and spoke with his counselor. He did not know of the things she had endured, and she was not sharing. She wanted him well. She talked to her sister Leronis often. She was aware.

One month while she visited JoAnn, Denise came along for the weekend. I joined them while Jean watched the boys for me, and Jo's sons were with their dad. We had a girl's night. We had not done so since Tony's death, and we were overdue. It felt good. This time was different. Our mom talked intimately about her life. It was a first. She talked about her early childhood through her adult years. We listened, holding on to every word and asking questions. She did not act as though we were prodding or intruding, but answered every question. We were surprised; it was unexpected. We laughed at her a lot. Some things were funny. She could take it, she laughed too. It was seeing her for the first time as a child, teenager, and an adult. She shared the things unpleasant that happened to her. At last we saw the secret reasons for her womanhood.

She shared life—the good and bad of it, mistakes and some very private glimpses that she could have kept hidden but chose to disclose. She had not become bitter or stayed humiliated. She said, rise above misfortune and learn to laugh. Unity and family were important encouraging us to be fair with people and forgive. Realize and admit our imperfections, be honest, follow our hearts. Allow nothing to destroy our love for life and each other. Distinguish between love and lust. Learn our limitations. There were things she wanted to do but did not. We were proud of her. She was a survivor when she could have given up or allowed emotions to define her. She learned to take her bucket of tears and pour it in a flowerbed so something positive could grow from her experiences. It was not easy to be positive, but it was necessary. She fought for her self-esteem and decided to be her own person. We were very proud of the woman that emerged.

We talked all night long. We laughed about dating, television shows, personalities, shopping. We talked about important things and irrelevant things. We laughed until our stomachs hurt and tears ran down our faces. Denise, Jo, and I admitted things of our youth, things we blamed each other for so that we did not have to endure the pain of chastisement alone. Some things we were oblivious to until the confessions to Mommy. We were like, "That was you? You did that?" Pardoning each other, we laughed until morning, and we were exhausted. It was so much fun. Later that morning we ate brunch while reminiscing about the night before.

Exhilarated, not sluggish, Jo and I prepared to see our children. Mommy and Denise still had time to visit other relatives before returning to Maryland. We laughed as we hugged getting in cars and driving away. It was one of the best grow-up times we had ever had. It was priceless.

I decided to do as Mommy and Jean suggested, visit Phillip in Kuwait for two weeks. Mommy and Jean came to Virginia Beach to stay with the boys during school Christmas break. They were gracious enough to keep the boys in my absence. They made plans to enjoy their visit. I left two days after Christmas and school was scheduled to resume before I returned home, but they would be with the boys. It was a perfect plan, another honeymoon. Phillip said Kuwait was different. It was but refreshing. We had the evenings together after work. It was great on many levels. We toured Kuwait as he explained the sites. They were rebuilding a nation. Soon it was time to return home. Life changed quickly. One moment a great time and laughter, the next moment I was at the hospital. I had just returned from Kuwait.

It was the start of another year, and I was excited on the flight home anticipating the New Year. Phillip asked me to think about moving to Kuwait for a couple of years. I had even considered it for a moment. We had such a great visit together. I tried to process the thought of being there with Phillip and the boys. I knew the grandmas would not agree with the idea. I was not crazy about the idea myself, but I just enjoy being with Phillip and remembered how easy the boys adapted to locations. This was too far away right now. Mommy was healthy now for about two years. Jean was fine too. Still I knew they would not want us in a dangerous place. I was undecided. It had only been a thought. I was over it and ready to get back to life at home.

When I arrived, Denise and Jo met me at the airport. They arrived without children or grandmas. This was unusual. I dismissed it though assuming the boys were still with the grandmas. They changed the conversation a couple of times until I asked for whereabouts. It was obvious they were uncomfortable and by this time I had a sick feeling in the pit of my stomach. They said Mommy was in the hospital with a blood clot in her leg. The doctors discovered another problem after tests. My heart sank as they said further test were required. I wanted to get to the hospital as fast as possible. I wanted to see her, be near her. I could not breathe.

When I got to the hospital, Mommy was resting. She looked tired but other than that, okay. Her leg was slightly swollen and elevated. Although we quietly entered her room she awoke and started talking about my trip to Kuwait, Phillip, and how nice the hospital staff was treating her. I was glad about that, but she was the priority. She said in her very quiet way, "I'll be okay. Don't worry about me. You and Jo just take good care of my grandsons." I felt better hearing her voice and seeing her smile.

Months passed. Mommy had been in and out for the hospital a few times from the start of 1994 with one problem after another. She was surprised with new doctors and a new health plan. The doctor suggested Hospice services since he said it was a lost battle with the fight against cancer this time. He said there was very little he could do for her. We refused his suggestion to place her within a facility. She was not unconscious. She was alert and although moving slowly with the bandaged leg, still mobile. I did not grasp what he was talking about, the inevitable. Was he for real? Where was her other doctor? Why was he so glum? I started getting angry. She calmed me saying she was going to be okay. She assured me the doctor was only trying to help, and I should not take it any other way. I heard her, but I heard him too.

At last she was home from the hospital. Though Hospice was a beneficial program, we wanted our mother with us and were determined to nurse her back to health again. Denise rented a two-bedroom apartment. I drove up and stayed with her two weeks at the time to offer support in any way possible. JoAnn stayed a day here and there and weekends. We immediately started with a plan of action. Denise's friends helped during the week when she needed to run errands.

Family and friends outside the D.C. area did not know the seriousness of her condition at first. It happened so fast. My head was spinning. I would not say what the doctor said. It was horrible to my ears and even worse in my heart. Mommy said she rejected his words but looked very sad. I knew she heard him and searched for hope as he offered none. We shared with some of the family and decided to let them share the news because we simply could not say Mommy was losing a battle she did not know she had to fight again. When folks heard the news, calls and visits began almost immediately.

As Denise, Jo, and I gathered often in Denise's bedroom we talked about health care and how we would continue to provide for Mommy since she needed a nurse to help out until she was up and about. We settled on a plan. We all agreed and wanted to discuss it with Mommy, but the Dennis the Menace movie was on television, and she wanted to see it. We wanted her to see it. She loved that aggravating boy, and we loved to hear her laugh at his antics. She sat up in bed with the armchair pillow at her back and laughed galore at that movie. We popped in her bedroom at times to catch a scene of the television show, talk about it, and then back to our tasks at hand.

Mommy was getting better and moving about in the wheelchair. Although not happy about her looks, she spruced up now and again and seemed to feel better when she did. It was easier to keep the leg elevated with the wheelchair, and it was painful to walk. The wheelchair, though not the way I wanted to see her move about, was such a blessing. She moved freely from room to room taking her time and taking care of her needs. She seemed relatively happy, and it was springtime.

Suddenly she lost her strength and was unable to wheel about. She lost mobility. Later her morale declined with her appetite. She did not want to eat although we insisted. We battled with ourselves trying to cheer her as she rejected our parenting her. She was in quite a bit of pain. It was more comfortable to rest in her bed than to try and move about in a wheelchair from room to room as done so easily only weeks before. The pain was severe with little relief from the medications.

Phillip was in constant contact with me. He called almost every other day requesting updates. I blocked out anything and everything negative. There seemed to be many movies on television with severe illnesses. I did not want to see them, and Mommy agreed. I wanted to re-create two years ago when we went through this and came through victorious. I wanted to re-create the time, the people, the surroundings, and I wanted to have Mommy come through the storm again as she did previously. Mommy talked less, but she insisted she was okay.

That summer brought many changes as school ended for the boys. They were six and eight years old. We packed and stored our household goods, moved from Virginia Beach back in with Jean. The boys and I were planning to move to Kuwait with Phillip after Mommy got better. As I traveled back and forth during the summer, I took the boys with me fewer times than in the spring. They asked questions and I answered that she was sick. They wanted to be with her and make her feel better. I explained briefly as I drove along that she would be lying down resting a lot as opposed to up and about in the wheelchair as they had seen her only a week before. They were not afraid of the wheelchair. They thought it was cool, so while Mommy sat on the sofa, they were in the chair wheeling about the room. There was a big difference in the way Grandma Yvonne was acting now. They talked to her as she encouraged all of her grandsons to sit on the bed next to her. Jo's children were there as well and we were nervous that they would hurt her laughing or playing while she lay down but they did not. They were very careful. She was fine with them around her.

As I watched the boys play and her smile at them, I thought about how much she loved us. I thought about our talks as well as the quiet times. I remembered her telling a friend how much she loved us and that we were her life. She did not make us sound like angels; actually, she was speaking of our misbehaving, but she laughed and said how much we meant to her. She said love was bigger than a feeling; it was a state of being. I smiled as I heard this. She seemed reserved and in a different mindset. I could not explain. Something was happening, and I did not like it. I did not understand or maybe I simply did not want to understand. Her demeanor was changing. We contacted Hospice and received a nurse for an hour a couple of times each week. I cannot remember exactly how often she visited, but the nurse was pleasant. She was kind and patient. She tried to make our mom as comfortable as possible. Most of the time while the nurse was with her, so were we. She was seldom alone for more than a few minutes.

THE LAST MILE OF THE WAY

When I thought of that day, it seemed so unreal. Waking early Saturday morning from a night of restless sleep, there was urgency to get back and see Mommy. I was at Jean's house and had only been back two days since my last visit to Maryland. I had taken Jean with me on the last visit, and we stayed with Mommy for a few days. Jean said she did not realize Mommy was so ill until she saw her. Mommy's voice was strong on the phone, and they spoke often. But what she saw in her eyes was different. I heard the words from Jean's mouth and wondered what she saw that I did not see. Nevertheless, I did not focus on it. Mommy's countenance had changed a little as though she was tired. I accepted that because I would be tired of lying in that bed day after day too. She had a right not only look tired but also feel drained. The fact that she began to show signs of pain and discomfort were totally acceptable. But now I was feeling a need to get back to her. I planned to visit that day anyway, but there was a need in my heart to go immediately. I got busy grabbing some things together in a small suitcase realizing that I may have to stay for a week for some reason. Jean voiced her concern asking if I wanted someone to go with me, but I declined the offer. I assured her I was okay hiding the feeling of urgency to get to Maryland as soon as possible.

I began the drive suddenly realizing I needed an inspection sticker that day for the car. I tried to work it out earlier, but kept meeting obstacles then forgetting about it. I stopped by several inspection stations that morning, but no one could get to it within a reasonable time. So I continued to drive and stop to stations along the way. Finally, a service station could get the work done that morning. I told the attendant that my mother was very sick. Feeling faint as those words rolled off my tongue, I shared the urgency I felt to get to her. The attendant was able to bump me up ahead of a few people giving me only an hour wait; I thanked him graciously.

Getting in the car to continue the journey I felt overwhelmed and started to cry. It was the first cry in quite a while, and I could not stop. I began to sing spirituals and pray through my tears. Thinking about her favorite songs and love for music I still felt powerless. I began to talk to God aloud.

The four-hour trip seemed to last for days. I was guided all the way by the hand of God. I know this because my mind was not on the road or the traffic. I passed milestones wondering how I got there. I understood why Jean offered to have someone drive me but it was much too late for that now. Looking up and focusing on the highway I noticed accidents along the way and was so thankful it was not my story; thankful I had not caused this harm towards anyone else.

There was an overwhelming need to be there with Mommy at that moment. I knew I was on the way but felt the need to be there at that instance. It was very unnerving. She was with me through so many things. She even helped me through things that she was not aware of because of advice she had given some other time. It was an extraordinary relationship.

I felt useless. She had given so much to me, yet there was nothing I could do but pray. It was my most powerful weapon. I saw her pain eased by prayer. I had to pray. I believed in the power of prayer, and I knew she did. After all, she was the example that drew me to God. She said God was there with an everlasting love to forgive, heal, and restore. She believed and so did I.

I arrived at Denise's apartment. I could feel a weight on my shoulder as thogh something was pressing on me. My heart pounded so hard and loud. While parking I prayed again trying to shake the feeling before moving any further. I could not go in Denise's house feeling like this. I did not want to depress anyone especially Mommy. Feeling a little ease, I walked up the concrete sidewalk wondering why I was so tense. Everything's going to be okay, I kept saying. As I rang the doorbell, Denise answered the door. She looked tired. Her eyes told the story of concern and seriousness. It was obvious something was happening, but I did not want to know. Greeting Jo and her family took only a few minutes this time as my concentration was on seeing Mommy's face. Jo and her boys arrived earlier that morning. Terence, Jo's ex-husband, drove them. He was a great help. Looking towards Mommy's room I walked down the hallway that seemed to get further away with each step.

Then I saw Mommy. Something changed since the last time I saw her only a few days before. When I saw her last we laughed until she cried watching the movie Denis the Menace, again. We talked about how he kept them on their toes. She laughed loud and hearty that day. I remembered our last conversations so well. Two weeks before we talked about her increase in strength, and she was sitting up in bed. It was new and fresh, and she wanted to make the most of it. Denise, Jo, and I were together and talked with her about getting back up on her feet. We were all excited. She had an appetite again. We were very positive. Now there was a drastic change, and she looked very ill. Her complexion had darkened.

Standing at her door, I could not believe my eyes. Her appearance had drastically changed. She looked very weak and fragile as she lay in bed. Now she looked bedridden. Previously she looked as though she were resting in her bed. I knew the difference. She had lost quite a bit of weight. I wondered what was going on. It was as though I was seeing a different person. What happened so quickly? I wondered why she looked so different. Denise said she had not slept in two days. She hardly recognized me. She turned to me with a puzzled look. We talked—or rather I talked to her. I gently called her repeatedly. My words seemed to have no effect on her. She was not responding.

JoAnn walked into the room and sat on the other side of the bed looking solemn. Stephanie and Darnley were there also and passed by the door not entering this time though they tried to speak with her. As Denise entered the bedroom, she told me that Jo had not left Mommy's bedside since she had arrived that morning, except for a bathroom break.

I brought my stereo box and a favorite gospel CD. I walked out of her bedroom into the living room to get them. I walked back to her room deciding to play it for her. She was unaffected by the music. She did not turn from the point that had her attention. Usually whenever she heard these gospel songs she sang and even cried with joy. But she was unmoved.

Immediately I knew what was happening. My mom was slipping away before my eyes. She was passing from this life to the next one. I called her back again and again only to see her slip right back to a place that was very peaceful to her. She spoke as though she had privacy or was unconcerned about what one might think about what she was saying. She called him by name. She was talking to Jesus. In awe, I moved from her bedside. I needed to be away, to think, to digest. She smiled.

Going quickly into the bathroom I closed and locked the door, and began to sob. I did not want to be disturbed. Closing the lid on the commode I sat down and wept with my face in my hands. My mother was dying. There I said it. I felt sick to the stomach. She was dying, and I had to let her go. I did not want to let go, but she had been in so much pain the last few days. None of us wanted that. I understood why Jo did not want to leave the bedside and why Denise said little. Our hearts were in harmony. I prayed again. This time I prayed, "Father, not my will, but thy will be done." I did not want her to lay there sick like that. I gathered strength, breathe deeply, washed my face with cold water and opened the bathroom door.

Denise met me at the door, and Jo was with her. I stepped back as they entered the bathroom. I did not want to talk to them, but I needed them. They wanted to be away from the children as well as the others waiting outside. We closed the door. Denise began to speak of the last strenuous forty-eight hours. She said Mommy was exhausted. She had not slept, was in much pain, and kept speaking of a faraway place. We said, no more suffering. We felt if she was holding on for us it was okay to let go and we began to cry together. We loved our mother so much; we did not want her to die. But she would not get well this time. I scolded myself for thinking the end was here. She could get better. In the presence of God, why would she choose to be on this side when we are living this life to get to the other side? This was our faith in God.

I walked back into Mommy's bedroom. Her conversations continued. I stood unafraid nearby to listen. I knew it was private, but I wanted to know what was going on. Her eyes were wide open, yet she did not see me. I called to her. She looked over to me and smiled this time but gently turned back. The scripture came to mind, "Come unto me all ye that labor and are heavy laden, and I will give you rest." Matthew 11:28. She was so tired. She looked at Jo and me and started talking to us. She was tired and ready to go to sleep. I had to talk to Mommy though. As she lay with her eyes closed, it was imperative that she know how much I loved her and how much she meant to me in that moment. Denise came in the room. I crawled up on the bed next to her and lay at her side. Jo followed crawling up on the other side. Mommy opened her eyes looking at the three of us. There were no more restrictions, no cautions, just us and Mommy. I stretched out near Mommy snuggling up onto her shoulder. Jo followed. We talked about how great she was and how thankful we were to have her as our mom. She smiled as we talked about Tony. We talked about the Lord, and she smiled again. We talked until she closed her eyes again. She continued to smile.

Finally, she was asleep. Denise walked out. As I looked up at her, I did not see sickness. I saw only Mommy, the sweet woman with whom I had the privilege of sharing my whole life. She looked peaceful while getting some rest finally. She started to snore. We smiled at the familiar sound. She snored even louder. Denise walked in again, and the three of us smiled at each other. There was such calmness in the room, then the loud snoring ceased. There was silence. Mommy was gone; so was her pain and suffering. She was at peace.

The sunlight beamed in through her bedroom window. I looked outside the window where children were playing and enjoying their summer day. It was such a beautiful day, and Mommy was gone. I commented that the world did not know such a gift to the world had just died, and time did not miss a beat. It stopped for no one. I felt overwhelmed with peace, then I looked at the bed where my mom lay and realized I would hear her laughter no more. I smiled at her and then tears gushed. I had to cry. The three of us began to cry aloud and seemingly in harmony. Sorrow swept over us as surely as the reality of her demise was present.

Shortly thereafter Denise regained her composer and reminded us that we needed to take care of those in the apartment with us and Mommy. Thank God for her disposition. We needed it to get us back on track and forward thinking.

Denise and Jo walked out the bedroom into the living room and talked with Stephanie, Terence, and Darnley. They helped contact family and friends to tell of our loss. I stepped into Denise's room and called Phillip while Jo and Terence talked with the children. We awaited the paramedics and the police. We thanked both for coming to ensure the symmetry of law and order. There was a funeral service in Washington, D.C. and North Carolina. Although Phillip had flown from Kuwait only two weeks prior to visit Mommy and make her laugh, he was back to say farewell this time.

Our dad was at the funeral in North Carolina. He stopped by JoAnn's almost daily before the funeral to check on us and express his sadness for our loss. It was not easy to say farewell, but we were surrounded by people who loved my mother and loved us. They consoled, cried, and laughed with us, and sometimes just held us in their arms to remind us that we were not alone. We mustered the strength to say thank you, or at least I think we did. We tried.

We were numb. Our mom was gone, and we did not want to feel. Nevertheless we recognized we still had responsibilities. We had to live. She would have insisted, and others needed us. We fought depression. Grief wanted to be our friend. Heartache wanted to be our buddy. Some time they were. Denise, Jo, and I talked constantly. We went back to our homes, and the boys and I prepared to go to Kuwait. I had to trust God for strength. Some days I gained strength from those two little guys who knew the perfect time to give me a hug. Checking on each other became second nature for my sisters and me as we tried to help each other endure this great hardship especially Denise. Her life had changed so much as Mommy lived with her and she was at her bedside every day. She was with her morning, noon, and night feeding, bathing and safeguarding her. Now she had a room, an empty bed, and a closet full of Mommy's reflection. It was a lot to experience. We had to check on each other. That is how Mommy raised us, and it was not a time to forget during this season of sorrow.

We talked about life without Mommy, but the thought of it did not sound right. She had to be there, but she could not and we needed to be present in our lives. We talked about family. I did not realize you could hurt so deeply. It was a part of the package when you loved so hard.

Three months later the boys and I prepared to unite with Phillip in Kuwait; it was a hard transition. The days of preparation weighed heavy on my emotions as I battled leaving the area. I joined Denise, Jo, and Jean at Mommy's graveside the week we were scheduled to fly. I felt as though I was leaving Mommy. My heart ached, and I cried as though her death was fresh to me. It was almost three months, but it felt like yesterday. As we drove away, we bid farewell to Aunt Leronis who had joined us at the graveside. I saw one of Mommy's cousin that resembled her. She was in a passing car. When she saw us, she stopped her car. We exited the cars to greet each other with hugs and kisses. She was very dear to us.

When I saw her, I missed my mom. They were almost the same height with many of the same facial traits. There was just something so special about seeing her. I was glad and sad at the same time. I smiled as my sisters hugged her and I waited for my turn. I longed to hug my mom, to hear her laughter, see her smile, and just be in her presence. She understood.

She resembled my mom and normally that was a great conversation, but this time was different. Seconds later as I reached for her, my hug was embroidered with sadness and sobbing. She knew and just hugged me with salutations and suggestions of not staying in Kuwait too long and staying safe while there. Apparently my sisters and I were feeling the same, but our cousin and my mother-in-law would not allow us to go to that emotional place. Instead, the two of them started talking about Mommy's five grandsons and my approaching flight and seeing Phillip again. A few minutes later she drove away headed home, and we did likewise.

A week later my children and I journeyed to Kuwait to join Phillip. Days turned into weeks, months, and years. I still heard Mommy's voice when I thought of her. I remembered her smile and hearty laughter. She was with me in a special place now removed from my presence but alive in my heart. She did not want me to grieve my life away. I would survive. She danced in the living room of our childhood home as she decided to survive. Sometimes tears flowed, but the joy was around the corner for her, and it rounded the corner for my sisters and me.

The joy was in our faith. It inspired me to get up in the morning instead of lying there when I was not sleepy. It reminded me that others suffered losses of the ones they loved so dearly. God gave me strength to embrace life without her just as she had done in her losses. She lived after she mourned. Her life continued after the death of her parents, sister, and the tragic death of her nineteen year old son. She showed me how to heal from loss, hurt, and pain. My sisters and I had to live, to find our joy again, and laughter. It would not be easy, but it was necessary.

Holidays have come and gone. I used to call my mom for her recipes on Thanksgiving and Christmas. I never wrote them down; I called her for the blow by blow ingredients and technique. It became a fun ritual between us. I called every year. She knew I would call early in the morning for instructions to prepare pies, cakes, the turkey, chicken potpie, and the turkey dressing. She was going to hear me ask her, pleading even, for assistance. And…I was going to hear her laughter. I saw her smile in my mind and heard her voice. No matter which state, country, or continent I lived, the request was the same, "Good morning Mommy, how do I make a sweet potato pie?" She asked why I did not remember. My response…"I don't know, Mommy. Tell me again please so that Phillip won't starve." She laughed again and again not irritated; instead, she talked me through it laughing as I suggested alternate ingredients. She knew me; I would try them if she said it would taste good. It was all for fun, just connecting with Mommy.

I missed that laugh and those talks. I missed Mommy. Much has happened in my life since that time. I have had good and bad times, used a lot of the advice I received from our conversations, and remembered her wisdom.

Mommy has been gone several years now. Her life was over at fifty-four. Though her life ended, her legacy continued. She cherished life and taught her children to cherish it. Though it would not be perfect, respect it. She always instructed us to take care of our family. I knew these were not kind words, but the measure by which she lived. She sacrificed and taught it so that we would do the same for our family. She taught us to be present in their lives: show up, be there for someone other than self. She loved family.

A great memorial to her is to live, love, and forgive just as she taught us and to teach that to our children and share it with our friends. Her last days were not with cancer; they were with us pouring her love on her grandchildren, speaking affirmations to her children, and showing love towards her family and friends. Though flat on her back, she did not pity herself. She did not like it, but she did not complain. She was not bitter for the misfortunes of her life or ours. In the end, she still loved with the life she had left. She relished it for as long as she could do so, and then when tired and exhausted from this life, she took a very needed rest, snored even. From the natural rest, she continued to an eternal rest. Cancer did not rob her of faith or the essence of her character. She was a phenomenal woman.

I believe the scripture in the Holy Bible (Romans 8:38-39), which says, "For I am persuaded, that neither death, nor life, nor angels, nor principalities, not powers, not things present, nor things to come, nor height, nor depth, nor any other creature, shall be able to separate us from the love of God, which is in Christ Jesus our Lord." I believe this. Nothing can separate her from him, and nothing can separate him from me. Since we are all connected, nothing can separate me from her. God's love is so big that when I actually think about it instead of the disappointments, I chose to forgive over and over again. Love taught me that. She talked so much about forgiveness. She knew I needed to hear it and learn it. She wanted me better not bitter from life's lessons.

The pictures in the photo albums on the family room table took me on the journey to yesterday; some events had been forgotten until the picture stirred a memory. All were precious memories. I smiled as I remembered. I decided to decorate the large table with the albums. As I positioned all of the albums on the table, it gave others the chance to look on and remember. We pointed at photos and reminisced. Occasionally we were so invested that we had to remove the photo from the album as we recalled the familiar story. Sometimes we laughed real hearty as the stories burst back on the scene with the flavor of the storytellers. I saw family and friends from many locations. And what showed up in every frame every time...love. I appreciated the love and laughter; it was good for the soul. Loss drained physical and emotional strength, but laughter was invigorating, uplifting. It was like a cool drink of water on a hot summer day—refreshing.

Just like other families my family experienced love, disappointments, marriages, divorces, births, deaths, and the grace to keep living and moving forward. I learned through my youth, innocence, ignorance, and at last maturity, to be thankful for the time we have with our loved ones, however the duration. Some relationships last longer than others, all are purposeful.

I try to remember when someone I love and cherish is going through some of life's dark moments, reach out and send love their way. Time passes quickly and regret hangs around too long reminding of what could have been done.

Mommy hated to say the word, goodbye. She said it meant separated forever, and she simply did not like that idea. Whenever we parted for a while regardless how long it was we never said goodbye. We always said see you later. If we said goodbye, she quickly changed the sendoff. She said we were not going to part because we were forever connected. We did not see the significance as children, but it was very important to her, so we gave it respect. Eventually, it became important to us also. Even with death we did not say goodbye; only see you later because we knew we were forever connected.

As I close this page and chapter of my life with Mommy in mind, I encourage you to experience God's love, enjoy your life, family, and friends. Remember the good and laugh a lot. I bid you all farewell as profoundly as I know how: *See You Later, and God Bless You.*